The Pot and Other Stories

Stories of the 6th FEMRITE Residency
for African Women Writers

Editor: Ellen Banda-Aaku

FEMRITE - Uganda Women Writers Association

P.O. Box 705, Kampala.

Tel: +256 414 543943 / +256 772 743943

Email: info@femriteug.org

www.femriteug.org

ISBN 978-9970-480-05-0

Cover design: Asiimwe Bonnetvanture

Book Layout: Ronald Ssali

Printed by:

The Pot and other stories

FEMRITE PUBLICATIONS LIMITED KAMPALA

Word from the Editor

It was a pleasure to work with the women whose stories appear in this anthology. *The Pot and Other Stories* is a compilation of African women's voices, some seasoned, some new, all varied and vibrant. The stories present vivid pictures of life from different perspectives through engaging and believable characters. Covering themes raging from grieving, to corruption, to identity, these skilfully crafted stories are told in fresh, candid voices. The protagonists in the stories range from a young, ambitious, chiefs' errand boy in a village in Uganda, to a lonely, wealthy, dreamless, 70 year woman in the city of Accra.

The captivating stories in this anthology will take the reader through an enthralling journey as the protagonists in these stories navigate the challenges of life and death.

Ellen Banda-Aaku
Author of *Patchwork*

The 6th Regional Residency

FEMRITE greatly appreciates the partners who supported the Residency for African women writers held from 13th to 23rd March 2015. The 5th Residency was funded by The Swedish Institute and the African Women's Development Fund and it was implemented in Partnership with Karavan, a quarterly Literary Magazine based in Sweden. Special recognition to; Katrine Larsen and her colleagues at the Swedish Institute for the importance they attach to culture as one of the major pillars for development and Theo Sowa the Director of African Women's Development Fund, an institution that works towards the emancipation and empowerment of African women. The residency is part of FEMRITE efforts to build a sustainable network of African women writers' initiatives across the continent aimed at contributing to amplifying African women's voices beyond national boundaries.

We recognise the immense contribution of the different teams which made the residence a memorable experience.

The authors whose literary experience filled this pot of stories, from Uganda, Ghana, Botswana, South Africa and Niger.

The mentors who gave and did everything within their means to support the writers; Kerstin Norborg, Ellen Banda-Aaku and Erik Falk.

Residency Coordination team; Birgitta Wallin (also mentor), Juliet Kushaba and Hilda Twongyeirwe.

This year's Residency was held at The International Centre for Writers and Translators, situated on a quiet Island on the Baltic Sea, within the walls of the medieval town of Visby. We are grateful for the enormous support and contribution of the Director of the Centre; Ms Lena Pasternak. These stories are African experiences shaped by the peaceful and quiet centre and the long walks with Lena on the Island.

The Baltic Centre for Writers and Translators is an international centre for writers and translators established in 1993. It is a non-profit organization, a culturally rich centre that provides space for literary professionals to meet and work together and to host seminars and other projects including an annual poetry festival. The centre is financed mainly by the Swedish Arts Council and the Gotland Municipality and it is open to all literary professionals although priority is given to those from the countries of the Baltic Sea and Scandinavia region.

We value the unreserved contribution of Ellen Banda-Aaku, the Editor of this anthology.

Hilda Twongyeirwe
Executive Director
FEMRITE – Uganda Women Writers Association

Word from Karavan

The night is clear. The sea rolls its waves around the small island and the sky is dark. It's only six o'clock and it is rather chilly. In a room at the writer's residency at the Baltic Centre in Visby an alarm-clock suddenly rings. A young woman gets out of her bed and wakes her friends. They run out into the street and look up in the sky. For a short while the sky is lit up with radiant rays and arcs, fluttering curtains and smoke in different colours; the night is filled with dancing lights.

When the women get back to Kenya, Ghana and other home countries they will tell about something they never have seen before: Aurora borealis, the northern lights.

In March 2015, ten writers from eight different countries gathered in Visby, the small city situated on the Swedish island Gotland, for a ten-day residency that marked the third collaboration between Uganda Women Writers, FEMRITE, and the Swedish literary magazine Karavan. The place was not the usual one. Two previous residencies had been successfully held in Uganda, but this time several factors combined to force the shelving of our initial plans for a residency in the autumn of 2014. In the new circumstances we tried to turn necessity into virtue, toyed with the idea of relocating to Sweden, and found a great friend in Lena Pasternak who offered the

Baltic Centre for Writers and Translators to us. And so, in the stillness of Visby off-season, our little crowd took all of the rooms at the Centre, enjoyed intense working sessions within its walls, and slipped out into the silent streets a town full of ruins for walks or coffee.

Whether the Gotland air worked its way into some of the stories in this collection is difficult to say; the conversations about books, films, current events – and writing, of course – that contributed to the atmosphere at the Centre certainly embraced the world. What is clear, however, is that the residency proved a memorable event, that committed writers were given time to work on their texts, and that new writerly bonds were formed between participants far from their respective homes. The relationship between Karavan and FEMRITE, made several years ago, deepened further, and it is with joy that Karavan looks upon its collaborations with FEMRITE as parts of a real friendship between organisations. We are also very proud to take part in a project which makes space for new, important voices.

Erik Falk & Birgitta Wallin

Contents

Tina Shot Me Between the Eyes

Antoinette Tidjan Alou

Tina shot me between the eyes. I should have seen it coming, but I hadn't; in an epiphany of red, I discovered that I had gone too far. Then pain too, went away as I gushed out, was catapulted up and away from my body. In a state of shock, I resisted the blue light. I could not leave. I hovered obstinately above the scene.

I linger still.

It is Tina who arrests me. I wish I could ask her why she did that. I wish I could tell her it's ok. That I don't mind, really, that I only want to understand. But although I am close enough to reach out and touch her, she too has moved beyond me. The scales have shifted. I am here and not there. I can no longer influence her or rough her up or gentle her or persuade her or do anything either for or against her. She has become strong and alone and unfathomable.

She is frozen now. Standing. Her hands are hanging by her side. The gun is still in her hand; a pretty, feminine, lethal little thing. Tina does not curl up in a corner, hunkered down on the fluffy bedroom mat like she used to when I would hit her and call her names – all the names in the book. All the names except the ones that were silent in my heart, or stuck at the back of my throat. All the names of Tina like a thick coating on my slow tongue. All of her names that would not slough off like a sordid confession. A confession of weakness; "I love you Tina, baby, kitten, so take this and this!"

Tina is brown and thin all over except for her face, which is sharp and soft at once. Sharp in the centre, soft in the cheeks, strangely rounded on either side of that pixie nose, that pointed chin, those piercing dark eyes that ignite when she laughs or teases. For she used to laugh and tease. Sometimes.

The light is gone out now and she is pale. But she is not crying. She moves and sits on the bed.

I'm a mess on the floor. My blood and brains all over the place. I look like a soft-boiled badly exploded egg, but without the pretty gold yolk. My eyes are still there, wild. My small mouth is wide open in shock. I'm on my back, splayed. It's kind of funny.

I miss Tina already. I want to caress her cheeks. The cheeks I had learnt to slap. To enjoy slapping. But I find that I can't. It's the only thing that bothers me. That and how we got here in the first place. Why she lost it. Why she did it. How?

But she isn't looking at me. She is staring at the wreck in the bedroom. This is like a dream where anything goes. Not a bad dream, really. But, in truth it is not a dream at all. I can see that. I will never again be able to wake up and touch Tina's face in anger or love. For I loved her, you know. I really did. But I too, lost it.

It did not happen all at once. No. Once, life was almost perfect. Not quite, but that was because of Tina. It is as if her nature could not absorb perfection, so she drew a line delineating how much happiness she could admit. I accepted her strangeness, having decided that it was part of her charm.

I am not sure how Tina and I got together in the first place. I do not understand it even now as my life, or rather hers, flashes in front of me. Flashes in front of me, isn't quite right, but I can't pursue that now. It's not a flash. The shot between my eyes was a flash. This something I am experiencing is different. And I am right inside it, fading, but attracted still. Two black shiny magnets hold me here. They pull me in, irresistibly. I do not try to resist. I do not want to.

There is deep insight now. Speed, but no fury. No rush. A flash of visioning where time is no longer the thing that counts. Now; a time where things happen otherwise, the weighing up, now that weight and density have gone. It's calm. It's all there. Tina and I, throughout the years, though years no longer count. Though...

It was at the Young People's Retreat at Oberlin. Everybody in the Community called it the Singles'

Retreat. The name was supposed to be a secret. It was a very infectious one, like so many other things in our Community, *their* Community, where it was almost impossible to keep anything to yourself. How Tina got to be a member in the first place is a mystery in itself. She is pious but also very private. Not overflowing and warm like most of the sisters and brothers. You can tell that from the way she smiles, the way she hugs. The opposite of Larry's bear hug or Sondra's soft breasts melting against your chest for all of thirty seconds' hugs.

I had tallied it many a time. It was not only because I am a people watcher; not only because the Community was a lovely zoo. I say 'was', not because it has ended, but because after a while I couldn't take it and left, sick of all the holiness and all the togetherness. The family days. The prayer chains. The Young People's outings. It was at one of those that I first started to think about Sondra and to notice whom she was hugging and for how long.

She was warm and regular, Sondra-Miss-Thirty-Seconds, and sweet and innocent, too. Did I eventually decide that she was not my type? Did God? Or was it Colin, now her husband, or Sondra herself, who had taken fate in her hand? Who had sent me hunting for another potential mate in the small woods of the Community? Did I at some point decide that Tina was my type? Had she ever been my type?

Tina was nothing like Sondra. *Is* nothing like Sondra, not that I know what Sondra is like, really. I simply mean that I didn't know Sondra that well in her daily life. And, soon after Colin got into the picture, I started watching Tina instead.

The Community was large enough, over three hundred regular members, but few of us shared a roof and people went to different churches to leaven the dough of the world with the witness of their lives through the gifts of the Spirit. No one said it in these words precisely, but we all knew the mission and the expressions.

The Community was kind of endogamous though, so dating opportunities were not many. Finding your sort was no easy deal either, except where religious fervour was concerned. The Community encouraged hotness since God abhors the lukewarm. He is passionate, an extremist who prefers the Saint or the Sinner. Fire or Ice.

So, while there were many fiery females, a match was not easy. Married, engaged, too young, too old, already dating, not attractive, not interested, too new to the Community, not yet tested by fire. But there was Tina. Tested. Proven. Single. Not dating. Right age. But strange. Was I interested, and maybe more importantly; could I interest her, become the man in the Community whom she would finally find arresting after all her years of membership?

It's not just Tina that was strange, the situation was too, for here I was contemplating courtship without the conviction that the lady was my type and without any idea of what profit such a venture, if successful, would be. I had hit on her through a process of elimination rather than one of choice. I guess it was just the time of life, a longing for earthy roots even as I strove for heaven.

I played the guitar at Prayer Meetings; Tina was part of the Worship Team and sang in the choir. We sat not far from each other, but never together. Never. Not even after we were engaged then married. In fact, Tina and I never ever sat together in church except on the day of our wedding. We were always too busy serving on this or that committee. Serving. Saving lives. Exchanging a few smiles.

It was at Oberlin that I first watched Tina laugh. Oberlin of the Vale, Oberlin of the Flame Trees, of the Orange Groves. Cool and sunny, buzzing and fragrant, serene and earthy. Oberlin. Our Retreat Place. Oberlin, where I first saw Tina laugh and laugh, pulsating under the flowering orange trees with all of her body, all of her soul. Oberlin, where I first watched Tina grow from a thin quiet form, to the most substantially living vision that had ever blessed my sight.

I had no idea what had tickled her so, but there she was spouting laughter, moist and vibrant in the sunlight. I drew closer to her, suddenly possessed. I strained to join the circle around her. I wanted to enter it; the circle, her laughter. I wanted to enter Tina through the gateway of laughter. Immediately, I knew that I had to have her. In my life. In my apartment, barely furnished but paid for in full, with a large sunny balcony and sad spathiphyllia in mouldy terracotta pots. Did Tina of the crimson glee have a green thumb? Right there in Oberlin, I was ready to bet that she did, that she possessed every gift and grace and fruit of Spirit and Earth. My Tina. My Own. From that day and forever.

Forever, the time of the Community. No abstraction at all. The Kingdom had come, the Deliverer had come. Emmanuel was with us, God for us, forever, in us, with us, through us. Eternity was happening now and onwards, ever onwards till the glorious meeting of every nation and tongue.

That day, too, would see birth and glory and trial. Birth.

I wanted it. To bring forth, through Tina. A child of my loins; of her womb.

I feared that word of flesh and blood and filth, but above all I desired it.

I was ready for courtship, for marriage, for family. So, I wooed Tina. It worked.

Our flash courtship was duly assessed and approved by my shepherd, David, by Tina's shepherdess, Betty, by the Elders of the Inner Sanctum, headed by Vincent. Three months after Oberlin, when they announced our engagement to the assembled Community, I was there with my guitar in my hands, clutched as though I might lose it, and Tina was sitting on her chair among the choristers, occupying so little space. We did not stand together as prompted but merely bowed our heads to accept the benediction.

The Community took full charge of the planning of our marriage, leaving little for our respective families to do. The Community was our Family of God. We were in full agreement, Tina and I, but our families probably didn't see eye to eye with us in this. Mine did not matter so much, I was only the bridegroom, but for Tina's family, I am sure...

The marriage itself is hazy in my mind. If we can talk about a mind, in full view of my bits and pieces. They look ghastly but I can no longer clean. I used to be good that way around the house. But there is nothing I can do now about the mess I'm making.

Tina is hugging herself. The way she does when she is regrouping. The gun is now in the drawer of her bedside table. I watch her put it there, carefully. So that is where she had kept it! When did she get it? How? Why?

Her head is down, but she is still standing. Her chin is tight, fighting back. Making a plan. I cannot touch her. I can. I am touching her, but she cannot feel it. I touch her chin; I try to make her look at me. "Tina, Tina...," I say, but she does not move, does not turn towards me the bright magnets of her eyes. They draw me in all the same, so I can see nothing else, nothing but her.

She is wearing her favourite tee shirt. Almost the same colour as her skin. A brown woman in a brown tee shirt. A wall flower. A criminal now. And I am the victim.

Tina flashes before me as on the day of our wedding. A slender brown woman in a white dress that is frothy below the waist. A thin woman. Sparse. With bare shoulders and no hairstyle. Her hair is too short to do anything with, she says, and leaves it as it is. She wears no veil around her virginal face. Only a crown of pale pink rosebuds, a creation of one of the sisters, Heather, made with roses from her own carefully tended garden. Irrelevantly, I remember winter thyme and sweet basil growing beneath Heather's kitchen window and her veined hands making postcards and bookmarkers with fine floral elements. Dried.

I do not expect Tina's delicate shoulders to be bare. I find the exposure disarming. She looks so small. Like a child. I cannot capture the fragrance of the rosebuds on her forehead, curled tight upon themselves like the tender fists of newborn babies, clutching their secrets.

I want the ceremony to be over. I want to be alone with Tina. To take her away with me at last, to sit her on my lap in the sparse comfort of the Ethel Room at Lethe, to nibble the soft skin below her earlobes, to lick the shell of her ears, to hear her sea song. I day dream about Tina's crimson song. As the ceremony drags on and on, I remember her laughing in the sun at Oberlin.

We are going to Lethe for our honeymoon. Lethe. Tina and I and the grey mist on the green river, in another valley. Half of the Lethe Valley belongs to my family; though none of us live there now, the property brings in an honest income from ecotourism. We had lived there, my parents and I, for the first ten years of my life, tucked away in the heart of the island. I have travelled some, for studies, then work, but after Oberlin, Lethe is my favourite place on earth. I will take Tina there so that she will come to know me. We will walk together in the misty valley where I grew up. I will teach her to make a body scrub with soft limestone. I will show her... But first, the ceremony. The reception. The speeches.

My hands have always been a little wild. Exuberant, I spill red wine, inadvertently, on Tina's queenly attire. Down the centre of the white bodice a large, dark flower blooms. Tina is not happy. Her cheeks are as smooth as a baby's bottom, but she is not smiling. We will not have good photographs. The Family of God smiles encouragement, I smile back for both of us. Nothing can spoil this day for me, I think. I swell with pride, treasuring the way she had said, "I do".

But soon I am no longer smiling. I had been happy, even after the mishap; happy that it would soon be over. That we could soon leave our three disparate families behind: representative members of Tina's family to the left; the Family of God, abundant in the centre and, oh surprise, my entire family to the right, complete with uncles, aunts and cousins, all present, a challenge to the Family of God.

There are too many people here. Too much music and song. Then dance. The opening dance. The many other dances. We dance, Tina and I. We dance and dance. With everyone. I dance with Aunt Ethel. She is as tall as I am and no longer thin. We waltz, a close and distant couple, her belly separating and uniting us all at once. She tries to pull me over to the right wing where my family is massed. I slip from her grasp, escape into the dark, trying to get back to the centre. But my flight is not fast enough. The past arrests me. It slays me on my wedding day.

I stop for a moment to check the time on my Timex watch. It has fluorescent hands. Tina's gift for my last birthday. It has an alarm that goes teet-teet-teet and prevents me from stressing about awaking too late for the Leisurely Quiet Time that is a must for all the Advanced Members of the Community. My Timex watch agrees that the new couple may now slip away. I wink at it in the dark. I know that Tina must be tense, fearing the hour of reckoning, of the consummation of our marriage. My own tension is of another kind. I had had a life before the Community. A wild life that I had only hinted at once to the Assembly, out of necessity, before my Baptism in the Spirit. I was not proud of it, and my family had never been aware that there had been another me. Another Stephen.

I'm advancing to the centre to get Tina. To take her away with me to Lethe. I am still in the gloomy space between the right wing and the centre. I can see my family, thick as thieves, drinking, chatting with their heads together. I can hear them; I can tell their voices apart even with my eyes shut. They can no longer make me out in my dark suit in the dark. I hear a strong, low rumble. It's Uncle Dan, Aunt Ethel's husband. Aunt Ethel of the blue Ethel room, the best room of the ecolodge at Lethe, a suite really, where I will take Tina.

Uncle Dan is peeved but reasonable. "After all, the boy is lucky," he says to a group of grumbling aunts.

My eyes are closed and I suppress a smile of sympathy for the boy he's defining with his moist meaty lips, with his potter's hands. Strange hands for a doctor. I beam with a smile of affection for Uncle Dan. Good old Uncle Dan, God bless him. In the dark, I almost chuckle.

But Uncle Dan continues, in his voice that no one ever interrupts, "We are wrong to resent them, you know. Although, we got him young, he never did fit in with us, not like he does with *them*. They have *really* adopted him, with no whispering about weirdness behind his back. We should have told him all along, before it came to this. Blood is a strange thing. He must have felt it in his bones, all along".

I hadn't.

But I feel it now, like a chill. It leaves me hard and cool and naked.

I fetch Tina, wordlessly. I do not say goodbye to anyone. The assembled guests smile knowing, indulgent smiles at our retreating backs, so close together, suddenly. I drive to Lethe. I never tell Tina. I never thrash it out with my late family. I say nothing. What is there to say?

I do not try to talk to Tina now. No sound forms around my words. I cannot reach her. There is nothing I can do. But maybe Tina should do something to make this end. She does nothing. She does not scream or cry or faint or call the police or cover my body. Simply, she sits down on the bed; slowly, compulsively running her hands through her no longer short hair, sampling the texture, a strange absence on her face.

She had not been like that at Lethe, on the night of our honeymoon.

On our honeymoon at Lethe I had been as cold as ice inside, but I had wanted to make Tina *feel*. Had wanted her to laugh and laugh as she had done at Oberlin. I had wanted her to cry out to the night at Lethe; had wanted her to want me, to beg me to love her.

It worked. For nine days and nine nights of Lethe, it worked marvellously, and I forgot for a while.

We returned to town, to my apartment, to work, to the Community, to life. To a life that gradually became impossible. But that was because of Tina, who was capable of only so much happiness, and because of the child that would not come.

Tina had green thumbs. The large balcony of our apartment sprang to variegated life. She brought the spathyphillia in; placed them in the soft light of the kitchen window. She changed the pots and the soil. She spoke about proper draining and not killing with kindness and smiled a knowing tender smile for their lustrous leaves. They rewarded her with indiscreet, scentless white flowers. Spathes, Tina corrected me gently, knowingly.

After Lethe, I possessed Tina wildly, relentlessly, but she would not cry out. At Lethe, she had begged me. After two days of teasing, she had been desperate, no longer afraid; she had been crimson and flowing. I taught her many things and she taught me a few; things she never knew she knew. We had delighted in each other, watching the changing river from our window in the Ethel suite.

Our marriage did not thrive in town. After Lethe, we were never two again, laughing together. In town, she never took me, never begged me. At the meetings of the Family of God, she would chant endlessly in tongues, tears rolling down her cheeks. I knew they were not tears of rapture. I knew that she was meeting frequently with her shepherdess, Betty to pray that God would open her womb to give me the child that I craved. I knew that she too craved. I read her face as she watered her plants and beautified her apartment. Her apartment, not ours.

Small as she was, she filled it almost entirely. It drove me crazy – the order, the beauty, the white walls, the bright carpets, the elegantly carved furniture from her family, her Indonesian rocking chair with delicately inlaid bronze flowers. It was too much, all of it; too much lustre and shine and colour. Too much housekeeping and fragrance and cooking. It was too full, all of it, except the empty room to which she brought nothing. I stayed away as much as I could. She never reproached me for it. She never said anything. Not to me. Never. She had stopped working, fearing that the stress of her teaching job at St. Patrick's Primary School was getting in the way of our family plans. The classes were huge, the neighbourhood rough. She stayed at home, but nothing came of it. Well, nothing good.

I used to call her several times a day as David, my shepherd, had suggested. Of course, I had told him about the change in Tina, when she had stopped responding to me.

"Women are a mystery, Stephen," he had said to me. "They need words like the soul needs prayer. Like God needs adoration. You have to keep wooing her. Tell her you love her in the daytime, or she won't have you at night."

"God does not need anything, David!" I retorted sharply, contradicting, then suddenly ashamed. For David had mentored me throughout the years. He alone knew my story. And he had never judged or rebuked me.

He laughed. "He does, too!" he said. "God loves praises, just like a woman! Check your Bible!"

I did not check my Bible. I knew it by heart. I never went back to David. And I stopped calling Tina in the daytime.

But late one evening at the office, Lethe with Tina came back to me. The memory thrilled me like a good fix. I called home, but Tina was not there. I said nothing when I got in that night, earlier than usual, but I called every evening that week at the same time.

She was never there.

I started watching her. I called Betty, her shepherdess. Tina had not been meeting with Betty for counselling, although she went to Community services regularly. With me. Each of us serving. Near. Apart.

It was at that time that the white walls of our apartment started filling up with paintings. White frames housing red, shapeless things. It was at that time too, that Tina started bringing home a strange smell. Like turpentine and damp woods. She was seeing someone. He took her in his workshop. He smeared her with paint. She could not scrub it all off. Specks and smears remained. Small traces on her cheeks, under her fingernails.

On the day I found out, I hit her. Hard. On the face, with the backs and palms of my hands. She cried out. It felt lovely – the sting on my hand, her cry, the percussion of flesh on flesh. I couldn't stop.

I stopped going to the Community meetings but continued to beat Tina fervently, like I used to pray. She never defended herself. She continued to come home to me, barren and besmirched. I chastised her. She cried out. I learnt new ways of hurting her. Of hurting myself.

She got used to the pain, it seemed. Her body grew tight and silent. She would hunker down on the bedroom mat in a ball. Sometimes, I would have to pick up that frozen foetus and put it down on Tina's side of the bed. She would lie there like a huge pumice stone, while I murmured words of love, "O Tina, Tina, kitten, baby," into my pillow.

When our marriage entered the Valley of the Shadow, I stopped going to church as well. Tina went alone now, to mass and to Community meetings and she never told on me. At least no one called or tried to counsel me. I have no idea how she managed them, the Family of God. How she explained the bruises or stains of paint. I continued to beat the hell out of her, but there was no pleasure in it now. No pleasure in anything.

Sometimes, Tina would remain frozen for an entire night. But she would untangle herself and rise in the morning to care for her plants and her home. For me too, because I was in it, in her home, and she never shirked her duties.

I understood her less and less. I feared her and I feared myself. I would die without Tina. Without her, our child would never come. I was breaking down at the office. Shooting up again, in the middle of the day. Beating the hell out of Tina at night.

She would not leave her painter man. Her artist lover whom no one mentioned, whom I never mentioned, not once; not even when I was hitting her. Not even the first time. She did not leave the Community or me. But she changed again.

She let her hair grow. A new look came into her black eyes; a look that defied me. She seemed to grow stronger, decided. Not content to let her suffer, her man was setting her against me now. But still, she stayed with me.

Well, she never left, but brought more and more paintings of formless red blobs into the apartment. They choked the life out of me. I chastised her. Routinely now, not hot and angry anymore, but vaguely worried, with what was left of my mind. Vaguely. Confused.

Sleepless nights gave ways to listless days of weariness. I was yawning all day at the office. Today, the company doctor suggested I take a month off to pull myself together. Or even a sabbatical. I left the office at noon. I did not take my things. I was not going to take a month off. I was not going to go on a sabbatical. I was going to go home to Tina and beg her to forgive me, to help me. I could not trust myself to drive, so I called a taxi gave my address and dozed off in the midday traffic.

The little snooze did me a world of good. As luck would have it, Tina was there. Her mini Morris was parked in the first of our two spots on the parking lot. I would not have to hit her, I thought; we could talk today, like two normal people. Like man and wife.

The reek of turpentine and damp woods met me at the door. Tina was standing with her back to the doorway. She was putting up a new painting. A painting on the Mercy wall, the name I had secretly given to the only free wall in the apartment, right in front of the hallway. Why for Christ sake was she doing this?

I bellowed something insane, but she only turned and smiled at me and said, "Welcome home, Stephen. Do you like my new painting?"

It was the last straw! It was too cruel. Tina's mockery was demonic. To bring this here! This new painting was no red blob. The subject was quite clear. It was a portrait of my left heel, sticking out of a volcano; all that was left of me. I knew which foot it was because of the socks. I loved that pair of socks. The left foot had a hole in the heel, a big hole, but I could not bring myself to dump them and Tina refused to repair that old thing again. All good and well; but this painting...

I would not be mocked in my own house; over my dead body!

I lunge for Tina, ready to revive the old techniques that would make her cry out. But she does not hunker down and wait for me to hurt her. In a flash she is in the bedroom. I stumble after her, several paces too slow. She is already facing me, standing deadly still; the lethal little tool in her hands, pointed at my head.

Maybe I should have begged her then, but I couldn't believe it. I wanted to throw my head back and laugh and laugh, but dead serious, Tina fired.

I exploded in an epiphany of red. Too late, too late, I beg her. But she cannot hear me. And I cannot follow the blue light.

Cilia

Glaydah Namukasa Bwogi

Cilia crumpled the letter and tossed it in the trash can.

"Cilia!"

Cilia spun round, stunned by her mother's unexpected appearance in the kitchen. "Mum! You are supposed to be at work."

"What's the meaning of this?" Cilia's mother pushed past her and retrieved the letter from the trash can. "Do you know how many people in this world would die to receive such a letter?"

"I don't care Mum. I am not interested in Cambridge University anymore."

Cilia's mother edged closer, surprise registered on her face, "Cilia... you spent months working on the application. You spent sleepless nights studying for the... tests and exams, remember? What has gotten into you now?"

"I'll just go to University here, after all Uganda is the only home I have." She walked around the kitchen table to the fridge where she picked up a packet of fresh milk. She peeled the straw off the carton, inserted it into the opening and then swigged down the cool drink.

"You are joking, right?" Cilia's mother tossed her purse on the table.

Cilia emptied the carton and trashed it. "I will go to University here."

"Your dream, Cilia. It was your dream to go to University in Britain!"

Cilia wanted to explain to her mother that it wasn't just about going to University in Britain, but the whole issue was too painful to be explained in a few words. Ever since she had become conscious that her identity was a mystery, Cilia blamed her frustrations on her mother for not telling her who her father was. She did not know where her father was from but her dream was to go to Britain because all the dreams she had about her unknown father were set in Britain. Because Britain was her dream country of origin.

For years she had seen him in wild visions; lived with him in relentless fantasies. Every time she switched off her lights and went to bed she let her mind wander, sketching, painting and filling up would-be pictures of him; very tall, with a deliberate stoop that stopped him from hitting his head on upper door frames. Cilia toured the streets of London, bouncing in her father's protective hairy arms, looking down and mocking the children walking beside their mothers. At times she sat beside him in a boat, cruising down River Thames, admiring the Cutty Sark, Canary Wharf, the Tower of London.

Cilia slapped her head to push away the visions replaying in her mind. Then she pushed her hands in the back pockets of her black jeans and stared back at her mother who was staring at her curiously. She considered bringing up the subject about her identity once again, but decided she needed a long walk to sum up the energy to confront the stone wall safeguarding her mother's secret. Without a word Cilia turned away, dashed to her bedroom and yanked her white ipad from the charger. She stuck the earpieces in place to shut away her mother's voice now coming at her like a relentless siren. She hurried down the corridor, the cement floor chilling her bare feet. She went out through the back door and hobbled on the gravel to the front door where she had left her walking shoes.

*

Much later, Cilia returned to the distinctive aroma of smoked fish which lured her back to the Kitchen.

"Mum. Am I half Irish?"

"Here you are. Let's read it together." Cilia's mother hurried to toss the last bit of fish into the simmering pounded-groundnut sauce, ladled the mixture, and then placed the ladle on top of the sauce pan. She then picked up the letter which she had straightened out on the kitchen table and started to read it out loud, "Dear Cilia Ann Nankya, —"

"Stop it, Mum. I meant it when I said I was no longer interested in Cambridge University." She stepped forward and snatched the letter from her mother's hands and stuck it in her trousers pocket. "Am I Irish?"

"Irish? Why?"

"Because yesterday at Nandos I happened to sit next to a white lady who asked me if I was Irish. In fact she said I looked Irish."

Cilia's mother bent forward and opened the kitchen window that had just been blown shut by the surging wind. "You know that people have always tried to guess who you are; Ugandan-American, Ugandan-European, Ugandan-Australian, and now... Irish. Why is it a problem all of a sudden?"

"It's a problem because I have just been admitted to the most prestigious University on the universe and I can't go because I am a lost person. I don't have an identity. If I feel lost *here* how lost will I feel when I go to a foreign land?"

She waited, hoping for a response from her mother who said nothing.

"All I know about my father is that he was a white man. But a white man from which country? Mum I am tired of people smearing nationalities on me."

"Not again, Cilia."

"Yes again, Mum! Everyone else knows exactly who they are, where they are from, except me!"

"Cilia. Why can't we just celebrate this big achievement? You are one in a million Ugandan applicants who has been offered a place at Cambridge. Cambridge!"

"Ugandan-what? That's the question. This 'Ugandan' or 'African' identity works for the sake of demographics, for filling out school forms, for official documents and all. But not for me. Mum, I need to know my heritage."

It had been a while since Cilia had talked to her mother about her identity. When she was younger it was different. It was about her dreams to one day step on the grounds her father stepped, eat the foods he ate, and breathe the air he breathed. It had been the yearning to belong to him. To belong with him. To belong with her ancestors. But now, with Cambridge in the picture, she needed the truth of her identity more than ever before. The truth would give her the confidence to look the other students at Cambridge University in the eye and proudly declare, "I am a Ugandan with Italian roots. Or I am a Ugandan with American roots. Or I am Ugandan-European. Or I am Ugandan- something!"

"Mum, I need to know."

Cilia's mother measured a half table-spoonful of salt and poured it into the sauce. She stirred, and then ladled a bit of sauce on to her palm. She licked it with the tip of her tongue before adding more salt, She stirred the sauce once again, and then reduced the heat. "We've been through this before. I have nothing new to say to you," she finally said.

Cilia felt her heart bursting with resentment towards her mother. She simply couldn't trust her anymore. When Cilia was still in kindergarten, she asked her mother if she had a daddy, her mother told her she had one and that she would see him one day. In grade nine when she excelled in her Primary School Leaving examinations, her mother asked her what she wanted as a gift. Cilia said she wanted to meet her father. Her mother then said it was complicated. That she would understand when she grew up.

Now Cilia was grown up and it seemed her mother still didn't want to talk. Cilia realized she had been duped into believing her mother's honeyed words.

"I am going to University, Mum," Cilia followed her mother who was now walking towards the cupboard. "What more growing up do I need to do to understand the details about my father?"

Cilia's mother slipped the apron off, hung it up on the wooden hook on the cupboard door, and started out of the kitchen.

Cilia stomped after her mother into the dining room, "Are you my real mother? I mean…birth. Are you my birth mother?" Cilia shouted.

Cilia's mother stopped abruptly. She stood still.

"Let's face it, Mum. I am all very light skinned, all straight long hair… I mean, people call me muzungu. And you, Mum, are the typical dark-skinned Muganda woman."

Cilia's mother turned away and dashed back to the kitchen. She twisted the gas cooker knob to off with such force Cilia thought it would snap. Then she grabbed Cilia's hand and dragged her through the sitting room, down the corridor, and into Cilia's bedroom.

"There!" She positioned herself next to Cilia in front of the mirror. They both stood irresolute for a while, gazing at the arrangement of their images.

"There! The foreheads, Cilia. Look how our frontal bones push out of our heads. Look at the high cheekbones that define our slanting jawbones, and the v-shaped chins that define our oval faces, Cilia. What about the sharp noses? The folds in our necks. Don't we look alike?"

Cilia remained unyielding "Mum, you know what I want to know, and it's exactly what you won't tell me."

"Listen, Cilia–"

"Mum, just tell me where my father was from. That's all I need to know." Cilia felt her voice break when she saw tears well up in her mother's eyes. Whenever they talked about the subject, her mother cried. Cilia would then let it rest and they would hold hands and end the conversation. Often times, Cilia felt the bond between her and her mother could be stronger – if only her mother would tell her the truth –

"Mum…"

"I don't know who your father was, Cilia. Didn't know his name, didn't know where he was from." Cilia's mother spoke slowly as if the words struggled to escape her.

"How can you not know? I don't understand."

"Cilia!"

"Tell me."

Cilia's mother turned and marched out of the room.

Cilia stayed rooted in front of the mirror, anger and desperation scouring her heart. She pulled the letter from her pocket and straightened it. She stared at the Cambridge University logo, and then traced the contours of the cross with her forefinger. She had been made an unconditional offer. For a moment she imagined herself as a student at Cambridge but the image shifted quickly. She stuck the letter back in the pocket and lay on her bed.

The rest of the afternoon, Cilia lay restless on her bed, her heart aching with the longing to know the truth about her roots, and breaking at the possibility that she may never find out who her father was.

Cilia loved the solitude of her room where no one saw her smile back at her father. Where no one saw her tighten her arm around the pillow that served as her father's strong neck. Where no one saw her cry when she woke from sleep and the cherished images and echoes of her father's voice were erased from her mind. She looked at the stack of books she had read about Britain. They were piled on a table at the foot of her bed. As she lay staring at the books, the visions came back to her.

Her father called her, Annie. She smiled at him and listened to his fruity voice as he told her tales about the sculptures of the royal beasts: the lions, baboons, an elephant, a polar bear, how the animals were given to King Henry the III of England as gifts. She enjoyed the tales about the ostrich who ate nails, the royal games; how lions, dogs and bears were made to fight each other for the King's entertainment.

A voice came to her shouting piecing through the images, "*Kaatandise dda? Maama nasubidwa dda!*" Cilia sat up drowsy from sleep. It was Teo, the house maid shouting; she was back from the market where she had gone to buy vegetables for supper. "*Yanguwa wassubiddwa dda!*" Cilia's mother shouted from the sitting room.

They were talking about their favourite television show, *choti Bahu*. It would keep them distracted and allow her time to go to her mother's room.

Sneaking across the dim-lit corridor into the heavy darkness of her mother's bedroom brought an unpleasant taste to Cilia's mouth. She was uncomfortable snooping around in her mother's bedroom. But she reminded herself that she was only snooping because her mother insisted on not telling the truth. Cilia gritted her teeth and slowly opened the door.

She spread a groping palm past the door frame, over the wall, feeling for the light switch. The wide room gaped in disbelief at her sudden intrusion. The large, well-made bed stared at her with wide open eyes. Everything else, the zipped, red suitcases, the dressing mirror, the red carpet; all stared at her in startled unending silence. In the corner was the cot in which she had slept for the first seven years of her life. The photo albums were cased in the drawers attached to her mother's bed. Before she had moved into her own room, Cilia would spend time looking at the pictures in the albums, giggling at the photos of her mother taken in her youth. How easy it was, then, for her to open the drawer and reach for the albums. To open the pages lingeringly, and admire the faces of her mother's relatives and friends, and stare at the faces of white men with sweet innocence. It was only once that she asked her mother if any of the white men in the pictures was her father. "None." Her mother had replied, and Cilia believed her.

Now she couldn't trust her mother anymore.

She piled the albums on the floor. The same albums that once seemed so friendly and symbolized warmth and comfort now seemed to prick her with sharp-pointed protest, like the rest of the items in the room, demonstrating her unwelcome presence. She pushed shut the drawers, hoisted the albums in her arms, and then hurried out of the room. She closed the door behind her with her foot and forgot to switch off the light. She hurried to the privacy of her room where she started working through the albums. She pulled out all the photographs with a white man in them.

Along the corridor came the sound of clicking plates, forks and knives. Teo shouted from the kitchen, "Cilia don't expect me to warm the food for you if it gets cold. Even the real princesses in real palaces, sleeping in real royal chambers don't sprawl around in bed like newborns waiting for their mothers' breast milk. Once in a while they prepare their own food."

Cilia sat cross-legged on the bed and continued to examine the faces in the photographs one by one. Teo always complained about Cilia's 'fake royalty' life but what did Teo know? Cilia deserved the 'fake royalty,' after all her mother was rich. Her mother didn't go to university. After her senior six year, Cilia's mother got a job as a tour guide. Ten years later, she started a tour company of her own. At times Cilia felt her Mum owed her the royalty life; for bringing her into the world a rootless bastard: a polythene bag roaming in the air, whose origin no one knows. So for Cilia to wake up and find breakfast ready on the dining table, to go to the bathroom and find her clothes ready, her bed made, her school shoes polished, to sprawl in the back seat of the Toyota Harrier and be driven to and from Rosville International school was just a little bit of compensation for what she suffered due to her mysterious identity.

Mixed emotions swept through Cilia as she examined the faces in the photographs. Later she jumped off the bed, wiped her tears and stood in front of her wardrobe mirror. In her heart she knew she wasn't ready to give up her search for the truth. She promised her image that early the next morning she would go see her grandmother.

*

On the bus to Entebbe, Cilia surfed for information on her ipad until the battery run out and the ipad shutdown automatically. She read about biracial people, downloaded pictures of biracial celebrities. She dwelled on stories about people who were searching for their identities.

The bus conductor soliciting fares from the passengers ran out of patience asking her for the fare. He burst out, "You think we have never seen an ipad before?

All these people have phones but they can put them away for a second and pay their fares!"

Cilia lifted her face to find the conductor towering over her. "Are you talking to me?" She spoke in polished Luganda, which drew some chuckles from other passengers. The conductor laughed. *"Omuzungu amanyi oluganda."*

Cilia thrust a five thousand Ugandan Shillings note into the conductor's palm then she threw her head back on the seat and closed her eyes.

Cilia's grandmother hurried out of the house. She was holding a sisal mat, and a newspaper, both of which she dropped the moment she saw Cilia entering through the small gate. With pencil thin cornrows in her hair, Cilia thought her grandmother younger than she looked six months before, when Cilia last saw her.

"Am I looking at my miracle child? Is it my miracle child?"

For the first time Cilia was troubled by the words 'miracle child'. Would the answers to all her questions be buried inside her grandmother's endearing words? She fell into the offered embrace and burst into tears. "Please tell me everything is all right. That you are well and that your mother is well."

Cilia buried her face in her grandmother's bosom and cried tears that drenched her grandmother's red T shirt. When her tremors subsided, Cilia eased herself from the hug and looked at her grandmother.

"Jjaja, why did you call me a miracle child?"

"Is that why you are so upset?" Jjaja's voice was as modulated as always.

"You will probably think I am crazy, Jjaja." Cilia sniffled "But I can't accept my admission to University of Cambridge until I know my identity. I know Mum already told you about my acceptance."

They sat down in the shade of a Jacaranda tree; Jjaja offered her lap for Cilia to lay her head. Cilia rested her head in her Jjaja's lap. After a long silence Cilia got up and pulled her ipad from her bag then she remembered the battery was dead. "Mum doesn't know I am here," she said, "May I use your phone to text her?"

"Call her." Cilia's Jjaja reached for her blackberry which was tucked in the side pocket of her denim skirt.

"I will just text her." She quickly worked the keypad. "I took a bus from Bugonga to the City Square," Cilia said after she pressed the send button. "It was a disaster. People just don't seem to understand that... I am one of them. That I am a Ugandan just like they are. They look at me like I am a foreigner!"

"I am listening."

"I wouldn't mind what anyone thought Jjaja, if I knew my roots. I wouldn't mind going to Cambridge if I knew how I would introduce myself to my fellow students."

One at a time Jjaja picked the purple flowers that kept falling from the jacaranda on to the mat, and tossed them into the grass as she listened.

"Jjaja, I've never asked you about this before. Did you know my father? As in … did you know where he was from?"

Jjaja paused with a flower between her thumb and fore finger. She remained silent.

Cilia snatched her bag from the mat, flipped it open, and then extracted the five photographs she had carefully sealed inside an air-padded envelope. "Here, Jjaja. I got these from Mum's album." She quickly peeled off the seal and re-examined each photograph, her hands shaking as she considered the possibilities.

In one picture, her mother lay stretched out on a straw mat, her face covered with a straw hat that had the same red-and-golden patterns as the mat. The dress she was wearing had a long slit that ran up past her knees to her mid-thigh, revealing skin the colour of strong black coffee. Beside her was a white man resting on his side, his torso propped up by his right elbow. He was facing her. He would be staring at her face had it not been shielded by her hat.

In the group picture her mother was the only woman among ten men, three of them white. They were all smiling into the camera. "You may probably think I am crazy but … Is any of these men my father?" Cilia said, arranging the photographs in a row on Jjaja's lap.

Jjaja did not look down at the photographs. "Cilia, is that a question you should be asking your grandmother?"

Cilia considered the words for a while before she said, "I don't know. My mother won't tell me. No matter how many times I've asked her, she won't tell me."

"Maybe you are too hard on her."

"She owes me. I have the right to know who my father is. Why won't she tell me?"

"Maybe it's better that you just put the subject to rest."

Put the subject to rest? The last time they had seen each other, only six months earlier, when Cilia had told Jjaja she was applying to her dream Universities; Cambridge, Harvard, Yale, Jjaja had showed her approval with a clap of hands. Told her how important it was to never give up on dreams. How many times had she told Jjaja she had recurring dreams about her father? How many times had her grandmother promised those dreams would come true? So now how did she expect Cilia to just put the subject to rest and give up on her dreams? "Why won't anyone tell me anything about my father?"

Jjaja was suddenly laden with hesitation. "Because no one knows who he was."

"Was? He's dead?"

Cilia's grandmother bent forward and looked at her blankly.

The phone beeped. They both looked at it.

"A message from Mum." Cilia said looking at the screen. "She says I shouldn't leave. She is on her way here."

Another beep.

"She says…" Cilia looked up at Jjaja, 'We must settle this now. Once and for all.'

*

Mum says I have nothing to do with her unhappiness.
But I don't believe her.
It's my fault that I came out of her womb a WHITE beautiful baby girl when in fact everyone else, including herself, expected a BLACK bouncing baby girl.

Mum says I am not a mistake in her life.
But I don't believe her.
I was a result of the greatest mistake of her life; cheating on her fiancée with a white man she met on a road trip to Mombasa.

Mum says she never regrets having me.
But I don't believe her.
I am the result of the thirty minutes she spent with a white man she barely knew
I am the regret in Mum's life!

Cilia scrunched the piece of paper and threw it in her mouth. Cleary, her first poem shouldn't be her damned autobiography. What will her fellow students at University of Cambridge think of her?

It is Well With My Soul

Wame Molefhe

I was lying on the couch watching *Come Dine with Me*, Mama's favourite TV show, when I felt my phone vibrating under my pillow.

I pulled it out. 'Hospital' flashed. I answered.

"Miss Molao? It's Sister Ruth. You're needed at the hospital…Please." The nurse's tremulous voice always made me want to offer her a tissue or comfort of some sort.

I glanced at the wall clock. It read a few minutes before midnight. I must have fallen asleep because the credits were rolling, and I had no idea who had won. If Mama had been with me, she would have admonished me: "Tshego, the best place to rest is your bed."

There had been many calls at such ungodly hours when the hospital wanted to leech more money from Mama or needed my permission to continue to prick and poke her. After the last request, I swore that the next time I would stamp my foot and say, "Enough. Let God do His work."

As the nurse spoke, I heard a muffled voice in the background, and then she continued, "Doctor is with your mother now. She urges you to please come. Very quickly."

"Is anything wrong?"

"Please come. Very quickly."

Very quickly. Jarring words that I had not heard before – not in all the months Mama had been in and out of hospital. Those two words seared me. They lifted me off the couch and propelled me to the kitchen to retrieve my car keys that should have been hanging on the wall.

They were not.

The umngqusho that Mama had asked me to prepare, "With your own hands, Tshego," was soaking in a pot, waiting to be cooked. I returned to the living room, slid my fingers between the sofa cushions. No keys. I forced myself to think. I remembered I had used the toilet. I ran past the closed door of Mama's bedroom. I had not been inside there since the day the ambulance had raced her to the hospital. I looked in the bathroom but the keys were not there. I leaned against the wall and closed my eyes. I could hear her saying, "Take a deep breath, pray and retrace your steps, Tshego." So I did.

"Please, God. Please show me where my keys are."

I had driven back from the hospital, via the ATM earlier that evening, parked in the garage, deactivated the alarm, unlocked the kitchen door; then, dining room, living room…I remembered then. I had taken the money out of my purse and hidden it in Mama's Bible. Then I had shoved my handbag under the sofa before going to soak the samp and beans.

I raced back to the living room, lifted the sofa. My bag was there. I shook out its contents: tissues, a pen, a notepad, lipstick, perfume, her purse and a crushed cigarette pack.

Last of all my car keys clattered to the floor.

I ran out of the house. I was starting the car when I remembered that I had not activated the house alarm. Too bad. The dashboard switched on. 12:30. I had wasted thirty minutes searching for my keys. If only I were more organised, if I made lists like Mama…

I reversed down the driveway and on to the main road. The speed limit, red lights and stop signs did not count after midnight in Gaborone. Within half an hour I was running up the hospital steps to room D4.

*

I pushed open the door.

Your eyes were closed and the doctor had one hand under your chin. I think she was trying to press your lips together and I wondered if I slept with my mouth open too.

I looked at her.

She nodded. "We tried to reach you earlier… At least, Father John was able to get here before…He prayed for her."

I was sure I heard an accusation in her voice. I needed her to know that I was a good daughter, that I loved my mother, "I couldn't find my car keys."

I should've been with you, Mama. I'm so very sorry I wasn't. I wanted to pray for you, but all I could think of was that hymn you used to sing to me. *"Ke lapile ke yo lala..."*

I was singing when Uncle Vusi phoned. I couldn't talk long because the woman from accounts arrived with a stack of forms she wanted signed. Too numb to check each page, I scribbled my initials on the last. A text message beeped its arrival as I handed back the papers to the woman. "You just couldn't wait?" I asked.

"It's not me, mma. It's company-"

I held up my hand and shook my head.

She left.

I read my message.

MHSRIP. See you later. May the good lord comfort you. Sent at 02:04 by Aunty Rosa.

I guessed the "Have you heard about dear Nozipho? What a shame" mill was already churning.

I walked out of the room slowly, took the lift down to the ground floor and went to sit in my car. I don't know how long I sat there, listening to my thoughts in silence until a bird whistled, and then another. Sunrise. I remembered that I needed to get home. A car parked next to mine. Its driver ran round to open the door for his passenger. He helped a woman out of her seat. She leaned against him for a bit, before they set off towards the hospital entrance, slowly. She plodded, duck-like, from side-to-side, in that about-to-give-birth way women do.

Uncle Vusi's car was parked in your driveway when I arrived. Thank God it was him and not you-know-who. He was sitting on the rusting, wrought iron bench by the front door. He stood up when I approached, kissed me on both cheeks and held me close to him.

"She's resting now, Tshego."

"Yes, Uncle…" I fumbled with the front door key and it fell. I picked it up and blinked away the sting of tears, unlocked the door. We walked inside.

"Uncle Sizwe says he's on his way."

"Oh God. Already?"

"He's your uncle, my child and he cares for you."

And heat rushed to my cheeks. "I'm sorry."

Your brother is like you that way – able to shrink me without ever raising his voice.

"A cup of tea, Uncle?"

"No. No, my child. You look exhausted. Why don't you lie down for a while? I'll call you if I need you."

I shook my head. "There's so much to do…I must get things ready."

I was sweeping the verandah when Uncle Sizwe arrived. I swear he is getting worse with age, Mama. He hugged me. Too tightly. Adopting his very-important-person's voice, he announced that the family needed to meet urgently. Goddammit, Mama! I hated the way he charged into the house, like one of his Brahman bulls, wearing that maroon suit, the one with a permanent shine on the bum.

"We will need to map the way forward as per tradition."

Mama, who in God's name speaks like that? Oh God. I'm sorry, Mama. I really didn't mean to take God's name in vain.

Truth is that I was relieved your brothers were around to receive all the people who came by the house. Unschooled in the language of death, I was still searching for the most appropriate words to speak about it. "Passed away"– not "died". "At rest" – not "dead". And I needed to practise the stoic expression that bereaved people wore when those who brought comfort said things like "God never gives you more than you can carry".

Anyway, I listened to Uncle Sizwe say how you had deceived us all the day you died. "She sat up in her hospital bed and said how much better she was feeling. Then she asked Tshego to cook her samp and beans." His audience nodded. "She was saying goodbye."

If I had known how to recognise death's knock, I would not have left your side.

I whispered to Uncle Vusi that I had errands to run. He did not object. I thought then that nothing was more important than buying tea bags (Rooibos and Five Roses), sugar (brown and white), and milk (only low fat). You see, I *was* listening when you lectured me about being a good hostess and making a home welcoming. There had to be magwinya and tea to serve when people came by.

That was what I was thinking as I reversed my car down the driveway. I must have been going too fast because the tyres screamed and heads turned.

Walking up and down the aisles in the Co-op, I searched for your favourite brands. On my way home, I remembered that we didn't have an urn. And your church people hadn't returned your enamel teapots. And I had to start making the ginger beer because your recipe needed five days to brew. I swung the car round in front of the 'no u-turn' sign and returned to the shop.

As I was trying to decide whether to get one or two urns, a cuckoo popped out of a wall clock. It scared me half to death. I stood there for a minute wondering what kind of person would buy such a noisy thing – and so ugly too. That is when I realised that I had been gone for over an hour and people would be wondering where I had disappeared to. I went to the "10 items or less" till.

They still hadn't bothered to change the sign even though you had spent all that time explaining to the manager why it was bad English.

I was in the middle of the intersection when I remembered that it was a four-way stop. A car raced towards me. I braked hard and the driver stuck out his middle finger as he sped past me. I shouted: "You mean your mother, you bastard." My hands shook so much I had to stop. I needed a cigarette. Though there was no one to report me to, now that you were gone, I still could not light up in public. A combi pulled up behind me and honked me out of its way.

When I got home and wiped my shoes on your welcome mat, I noticed how frayed it looked. I noticed chips in the black tiles in your kitchen. All day people streamed into and out of your home and I felt like I was wading through mist. Faces of relatives and strangers merged together. From outside, I heard children laughing and wanted to tell them that happiness was not allowed at a time like this.

I felt like I was falling and falling with no one to catch me.

Father John insisted on conducting prayers that evening. I got out the blindingly white linen tablecloth and laid it over the makeshift lectern. When he had gone and most of the mourners had left, Uncle Sizwe was granted his wish. The family gathered in the living room so he could pontificate. His wife perched on the ottoman with her legs on the side table. Again and again, she glanced pointedly from her watch to her husband.

"This must not take too long. I'm expecting some visitors from overseas this evening," she told us.

"This won't take long. I will prepare the notice for the radio. I'll take it there myself. I know Dickson. He's in charge there...He'll make sure its read tonight. Tshego, you'll need to find pictures of her for the funeral programme."

Your people bombarded me with questions that I swung at, blindly, wildly. I decided that we would bury you on Saturday, and ignored protests about how four days were not enough to plan what was going to be a huge funeral.

"Your mother loved people. Everyone who knew her will want to attend."

I did not respond. I remembered flowers. I needed to order flowers, I thought. White. St Joseph's lilies were beautiful...No ribbons.

Uncle Sizwe asked about a funeral policy. Typical. I told him Aunty Rosa would probably know, but when your sister arrived all she did was bawl. She paused in front of the mirror by the fireplace to wipe her mascara-streaked cheeks while her daughter raced into the room wearing those thick-soled sneakers that I hate. Before any adult could shout, "no running in the house!" your very special crystal vase crashed to the floor. To keep all the words I had ever wanted to say to your sister and her petulant child inside me, I left the room. If I had stayed in your house a minute longer, I would have told Aunty Rosa her daughter was no genius and that she should just stop with the, "Go to your corner," crap and spank that child one-time. I might even have told Aunty Rosa that she should never have become a mother.

But I didn't say any of these things. I walked round the back of the house to your orchard and busied myself picking up fallen grapefruits and throwing them on the compost heap. I did not want anyone to think I was bitter because I had no children of my own.

When I returned to the living room, it was deathly silent. Your brothers were both shaking their heads. Chloe sat on her mother's lap, staring at the black ewe of your family. Dressed in figure-squeezing leggings and a boob tube, Aunty Beauty's only concession to convention was a sarong, tied loosely around her waist. I wondered how she always managed to show up at these family gatherings even though no one ever told her stuff. She had stopped by the bar en route to your home and was now drenching the living room in alcoholic fumes and strong perfume.

Uncle Vusi gestured for me to open the living room windows.

I went over to greet Aunt Beauty.

She stood to hug me tightly and whispered in my ear. "No one's going to bully you. I'm here."

Aunty Rosa said we had to have a women only meeting to decide the funeral menu.

Emboldened by Aunty Beauty's presence, I said, "No need, Aunty Rosa. I'm hiring a catering company."

"Caterers?" Aunty Rosa's shook her head. "Hm."

"Yes, Aunty Rosa."

"But your mother…"

"Rosa, leave Tshego to do what she wants for her mother. And anyway, where were you when Nozipho was ill?" That was Aunty Beauty.

Uncle Vusi held up his hand. "Enough! I will not allow this in my sister's home."

*

I did not cry when you died, Mama. My eyes didn't swell and stay red like Aunty Rosa's who, in between blowing her nose and sniffling, kept saying how important it was to express sorrow. She went all prophetess-like on me and said she saw years of depression ahead – wrought by bottled-up grief, a sort of hell on earth. I heard Mma D, our neighbour say that the new church Aunty Rosa went to in Nigeria had addled her brain for sure.

I laughed and immediately felt guilty, but the laughter burst out of me again when I tried to stop it. Mma D looked at me like maybe I also had what Aunty Rosa had.

The truth is, Mama, until the morning I took your Women's Guild uniform to the funeral home and found you laid out on a metal slab with your lips painted shocking fuchsia like you were a black porcelain doll, I believed God would perform a miracle and save you.

You would have been proud of me, Mama. I spoke to the undertaker like you would have done, gently, softly, in proper English: "Please remove that make up." Then I applied a fingertip of honey balm to your lips and dabbed a few drops of White Linen behind your ears.

You said to have faith, and I clung on to that, the way I did your hand when I was a little girl and we walked past the house with the Alsatians. Even when you stopped getting out of bed and became so fragile, I feared you might break when I turned you, I did not lose hope. When strangers accosted me in the street, in shops, at the hospital, to ask me how you were doing, I smiled and said you were getting better. Every morning I tiptoed to your room with a tray of rooibos tea and Ouma's rusks, expecting to find you already dressed in your brown leteisi, looking outside, humming "It is well with my soul." On Sunday mornings, your purple cape hung on the wardrobe handle, its collar starched-stiff; ready for you to wear to church.

Every day you praised God for nature's splendour, for your life, for your blessings. You even thanked God for giving you a daughter like me. I suppose that is why you named me Tshegofatso.

I believed it would not be long before we would sit in the living room together, watching *Come Dine with Me*.

For as long as I could remember, birdsong was your wakeup call and you always had things to do. You said Satan preyed on the idle. "We need to prune the marigolds. They look as unkempt as your hair, Tshego," or, "You must sweep the verandah and make your home welcoming."

But even though you obeyed God's commandments, even though you went to church, prayed every day, never drank alcohol, ate healthily, God did not spare you. I watched pain dig lines on your forehead and twist your mouth to one side. I watched you try to smile when the people from your church visited. I heard your whispered, "Amen's" when they prayed for you.

When I railed at Father John, demanding to know why you, Mama, he scratched his chin and tugged on his freshly-trimmed beard a few times. "Have faith, my child. It was her time," he said. "God works in mysterious ways."

I failed to suppress a yawn.

*

The day of your funeral Father John stepped down from the podium. No longer confined by the pulpit, he flung his arms to the heavens and paced from one side of the church to the other. Beads of sweat formed on his bald patch and zigzagged into the creases in his neck, and one balanced on his nostril before he flicked it away with the back of his hand. He likened you to an angel, pure and milky-white. Your pain was over and you had gone to a better place, he said. I thought maybe there really was something to this faith thing and perhaps you were right about church, Mama. But when we gathered around your grave and Father John got to the "dust to dust" part, his words yanked me from the clouds.

Those words signalled for men to get ready. Slipping off their dark jackets, they handed them to their womenfolk. After your casket disappeared into the grave, they shovelled the rocky soil back to where it had been removed. The awful clonking of the sods landing on the coffin made my head ache. They finished so quickly, Mama. Father John didn't have to shout first to instruct people to pitch in. Even the councillor, you know, the one who people say is too proud. Even he handled a spade, Mama.

There was a tiny girl there who sang in so powerful a voice, I thought it came from the big-busted, wide-hipped woman standing next to her. She sounded like you – much louder but so true to the notes. Around her, there were members of your Women's Guild. Someone thumped a beat as he danced. I doubt you would have approved of such boisterousness. I remember you saying that God heard the softest whispers, and the charismatic movement wasn't your thing, but the singers' voices stirred something joyous in me, swayed me: left, dip, right, and back in a smooth movement that would cast no doubt on the depth of my grief.

Yes, we sang for you when we buried you, Mama; mostly hymns in Setswana, a few Sesotho ones and three encores of "It is well with my soul", sung in your isiXhosa. I think you would have smiled the way you did when you realised you unwittingly drew attention to yourself. I can see you: eyes looking down, hand raised to your mouth to hide your slightly protruding teeth.

*

Picking my way carefully through the cemetery to place fresh flowers on your grave, I wonder, like I have many times before, if this place of unkempt weeds, decaying wreaths and shade netting grave-covers is our final destination.

Over in the corner of the grave site a lone council worker swings a sickle at the overgrown grass. "The dead must not choke to death," he says to me and shakes his head.

Since we buried you, a woman has been visiting me in my dreams. She does not cover her mouth when she smiles. Tears pour down her face as mirth shakes her body. I hope the woman is you, Mama.

I hope that you have found your heaven.

Ohemba

Bananuka Jocelyn Ekochu

So what if she is the chief's wife. He is too old for her anyway.
Ohemba thought to himself. He had always thought he
had everything he ever wished for in his life. He was
strong and stocky, with a dark skin that glistened in the
sun when he perspired, and muscular; a consequence of
the long hours he spent splitting firewood.

His milk-white teeth, embedded in a black gum,
prominently displayed because of his permanent smile,
endeared him to the women of the village. His image
was further enhanced by a pair of khaki shorts given to
him by a visiting white man. He had promptly thrown
his torn pair away, only to retrieve it when he realised
that he would need it in order to wash the new one. He
enjoyed being amidst doting older women and basking in
their praise and admiration. It was one of them, the wife
of the chief's herdsman, who had introduced him to the
overwhelmingly absorbing pleasures of the bedroom.

Ohemba was in a privileged position as the chief's errand boy; it meant that he was assured of a constant supply of good food and, once in a while, leftovers of the chief's local brew, tonto. His mother had always ensured that he was never in want, and indeed he never thought there was anything or anyone he could not have, until he came face to face with the chief's youngest wife, Mwangangye. She was the youngest and the most beautiful of them all.

Mwangangye! She was brought from her village to become the chief's sixth wife with much celebration and pomp. There was a lot of food and tonto for everybody. Prominent members of the village used the opportunity to show their support for their chief, by bringing all sorts of food for the feast, each contributor trying to outdo the previous one. The villagers took full advantage of the extravagant function to eat and drink as much as their stomachs could take. It was the utmost display of human gluttony. Singing, drumming and dancing went on for days as the village came alive with the kind of merrymaking that only a chief could afford.

Eventually the bride had arrived, surrounded by a party of dancing friends and relatives. Two young girls were brought to keep her company until she got used to her new home. She was also assigned two maids to take care of her needs. As a rule, in the chief's household, only the young women tasked with serving the new bride were allowed to see her, except her husband of course.

Other than the feast, Ohemba didn't think much of the whole marriage affair. The bride could not be much different from her co-wives, although she was likely to be younger. So whilst everyone was looking forward to the day she would be unveiled and presented to the public, he only thought about the food that would come with the ceremony. However, as it happened, when the day finally arrived, Ohemba was dispatched to the chief's second kraal because the herdsman had taken ill. He was instructed to take care of the herd until the herdsman was well enough to assume his role. Ohemba was gone for two months. When he returned there was no trace of the marriage celebration that had rocked the village.

One evening, a few days after he returned to the village, Ohemba entered the milk hut. It was a place where the women usually sat to clean and smoke milk pots and make ghee as they gossiped about everything and nothing. After milking cows, the young men brought the milk and handed it over to the women. The milk pots were then smoked using a special kind of grass. The grass was uprooted, cleaned, burnt and put in a small pot. A bigger milk pot was then placed face down over the pot with the smoked grass so as to trap the smoke inside. After a while, when the milk pot was filled with the scent of smoked grass, it was upturned and milk was poured into it. The smoke in the pot gave the milk a rich smoky flavour.

Ohemba had gone to the hut to pick a tin in which to collect the milk. As he was about to walk out, the tin in one hand and a rope in the other, Mwangangye entered. Ohemba did not need anybody to tell him who she was. It had to be the chief's latest wife. She was draped in a pink floral cloth and held herself in a manner that suggested she was the overall mistress of the chief's household.

In Ohemba's opinion, Mwangangye's striking beauty was that of a goddess. In an instant, he noticed that her smooth skin was flawless and her presence seemed to light up the whole hut. Even the black and white striped walls of the hut, which he always admired, could not distract him from her angelic light skinned face. He was so absorbed by Mwanganye's presence that the pleasant smoky smell of the milk pots, which usually whetted his appetite, did not make his stomach groan. Milk was the last thing on his mind. He could drink in Mwangangye's beauty and let the milk be served to the dogs for all he cared.

Mwangangye hesitated for a brief moment when she saw Ohemba, but to him the pause felt like ages. For a split second, their eyes met, and then Ohemba remembered to look away. When she crossed the room to sit down, he caught a whiff of her herbal ointment. All newly married women were given herbal ointment by their paternal aunts. It was meant to keep them highly desirable to their husbands. Ohemba lost his concentration, and as if to remind him of the reason he had entered the hut, the tin slipped from his sweaty hands and fell to the floor.

The sound was muffled by the grass, but to him it was thunderous. He scrambled after the pot which bounced in Mwangangye's direction. Ohemba mentally chastised himself for being clumsy. He hoped the noise had not startled her. He dropped to his knees to pick up the tin but he was not fast enough; Mwangangye picked it up. Ohemba jumped back to his feet and once again had to remind himself to keep his eyes lowered. She handed him the pot and in the process her hand brushed against the front of his shorts. As he took the tin from her he found himself trembling.

His mouth was so dry that words couldn't come out. Mwangangye smiled at him coyly and then turned away. She went and sat down on the neatly arranged grass mat which covered the floor of the hut. He wondered whether she had woven the grass herself. He watched her ample round bottom as she lowered herself onto all fours then finally settled on the mat. Her bottom seemed to be protesting at the restriction her wrapper was causing. When he had the familiar feeling of his shorts tightening around the loins, and he could no longer contain his massive excitement, Ohemba fled.

After his exit, Ohemba tried to make sense of what had just happened to him. He realised that he had just had an encounter with the most beautiful woman he had ever met, but he had not been man enough to say anything to her. He, of the legendary libido, praised by women young and old, had just been cowed by a woman.

Well, granted, she was the Chief's wife, but she was a woman all the same. And although he did not know how, Ohemba intended to correct that anomaly. Yet, the more he thought about it, the more futile it seemed, and the more futile it seemed, the stronger his desire for Mwangangye grew. However much he tried, he could not understand how the chief, so old and ugly, managed to find such a treasure. Ohemba could not understand women. The chief was very rich, fine. But what about the other side of things? What about the intimacy for example? Hadn't he, Ohemba, enjoyed wonderful moments with older women whose husbands were too old to satisfy them? How then could this young beauty stay true to an old, useless man?

That night Ohemba could not sleep. As he tossed and turned in his papyrus bed, he tried to conjure up the many times he had enjoyed the generosity of his women. What did they like most? His frustration grew as he realised that he had never actually paid much attention to what they enjoyed. All he knew was that they carried him on a cloud and showed him what heaven was like. This was another area of his love life that he had to change. When he finally had Mwangangye in his bed, he intended to make sure that she would never think of the Chief. Ever again.

He kept thinking about the way she had smiled at him, and a shiver went through his body as he remembered her accidental touch. Was it really accidental? Maybe she had already realised that the Chief was not going to meet her needs after all, and she was looking for an alternative. Who else was there but him? Hadn't the other women told him, time and again, that he was the most handsome man in the village? Surely Mwangangye must have seen that as well. Surely she must have heard about him. Suddenly he realised that he no longer wanted any other woman. He wanted Mwangangye. She was the only one worth of his love.

Ohemba knew that his love for Mwangangye was problematic. Although he was proud of his status in the village, his dream to acquire the greatest desire of his heart was extremely ambitious. As an errand boy, he was only expected to speak when spoken to. Even then, he could only respond to questions and not ask any himself. How then, would he ever profess his love to Mwangangye? For the first time, he doubted his mother.

Since he was old enough to understand, his mother had relentlessly told him the history of his birth, the injustice he had suffered at his uncle's hands and the events that had brought him to the Chief's Palace. His mother always assured him that he was special. The chosen one. That he would have everything he needed; which, in her own opinion, did not go beyond food, shelter, and the prestigious position of Chief's errand boy. She had told him that one day he would marry the most beautiful woman in the village and that, that day would be the happiest day of her life. Ohemba had believed everything she said, but now all that she said appeared to be hogwash.

Ohemba was an only child. His mother, Naku, was very old when he was born. She had been thrown out of her home when she could not conceive, but she had Ohemba eight months later. Naku was very pleased as she assumed it meant that she could go back and be reconciled with her husband.

A few weeks after the birth of her son, Naku set out for her matrimonial home, dreaming of the happy reception she would be given, because even if her co-wife had given their husband six children, all of them were girls. It was rumoured that he was planning to take a third wife, because he desperately wanted an heir. Normally the birth of a baby boy meant that a goat would be slaughtered, unlike the birth of a baby girl when a kilogram of meat was bought for the mother.

This time they will slaughter a bull because the heir has come after a very long time, Naku thought happily as she picked her way through the thick bushes of Kamunyama. She was about to pass the pond which was used to water the Chief's cows when she remembered that it was where she had first met the man that later became her husband. *It brought me good luck,* she thought as she approached the well. She bent and drew a handful of the anthill-red-soil-coloured water and sprinkled it on the baby's face causing him to scream in protest. *Hush, my son. It will bring you good luck,* she whispered. She chuckled when she pictured the look on Nyamwiiza, her co-wife's face, when she, Naku, finally showed up with the heir.

She will eat her heart out, she hoped. *Rweeha will not touch her for many days,* she continued in her thoughts. *What for? She has failed to give him a son.*

But as she approached the Palace, Naku's heart beat quickened. There was loud wailing coming from the village which could only mean there was a death in the family. *I hope it is not Rweeha*, she thought rather selfishly; *he has to see his son before he dies.* Clearly, Naku did not think that her husband would die. Life could not be that cruel.

However, as she entered the compound, Nyamwiiza appeared, seemingly from nowhere, and started hurling insults at Naku.

"You witch; you bewitched him because he chased you away. So why have you come?" Naku froze. It had happened. Her husband had died without seeing his son. Shocked out of her happiness but dry-eyed, Naku decided not to show her grief until she had given her co-wife a piece of her mind.

"You are the witch, Nyamwiiza. You have killed him before he could see his heir. You were jealous because I have given him a son in my old age."

By this time, people had gathered to see Naku and the baby, who was a spitting image of his father. Rweeha's brother took one look at the baby and dragged the bewildered Naku out of the compound. He claimed that Naku was a whore who had come to insult his brother with an illegitimate child. But everybody knew that he was after his brother's property and therefore wanted no heirs around.

Naku went back home swearing that her son would never need anything from his uncle. She would see to it that he had everything he needed. He would then grow up into a strong man who would protect her and bring her food and wild meat and a beautiful daughter-in-law and plenty of grandchildren.

When he was old enough to run errands, Naku presented him to the Chief because she believed that was what her son needed to be successful. And indeed Ohemba grew up a contented young man, believing that all he needed was his position as the chief's errand boy; until he set his eyes on Mwangangye.

When he could not eat or sleep for many days, Ohemba started to hatch a plan. There had to be a way of winning Mwangangye's heart. It didn't matter to him that if his plans were discovered he would be put to death for daring to insult the chief. All he knew was that he would die anyway if he failed to get her. He decided to make himself more useful than ever, and as a result, the chief found him to be more reliable than his colleagues. He therefore kept him around the household all the time.

Ohemba thought he would die of happiness one day when Mwangangye looked at him and smiled. He spent the whole day singing and worked even harder than ever. He started positioning himself in corners where he knew she would pass, and then he would hang about hoping to catch her eye. On a few occasions he noticed that she looked around as if to make sure that there was no one looking, then she would smile at him and lower her eyes.

Such days normally led to nights of fantasising. Ohemba knew enough about women to know that it was only a matter of days before his greatest desire was fulfilled. He knew he had Mwangangye in his sights. And indeed, one evening she approached him. "Ohemba, please carry my bathing water for me," she whispered into his ear. "And wait for me under the mango tree."

Ohemba could not believe it. It was all working out a lot easier than he would had imagined. Mwangangye had just confirmed her feelings for him! He ran and put her water on the fire and had a quick, cold bath himself, and then he rushed back to carry Mwangangye's water to the papyrus structure where only the chief and herself bathed. There had to be only one reason she wanted him to wait for her in the shadow of the mango tree, he thought. She was going to make him the happiest man in the Chief's homestead. No, she was going to make him the happiest man in the world. Pity he could not tell all those girls who would not indulge him, demanding that he marries them first. But it did not matter anymore. His Mwangangye was all he wanted.

He almost fainted with joy when he saw her figure fully covered in the familiar floral cloth, approaching. Dark as it was, he could not fail to identify Mwangangye's clothes. It was her alright. He had watched her enough times to be able to recognise her even in disguise. She didn't utter a word as she approached him with a graceful walk that only she could manage. She reached out with her hand and pulled him to herself. She held him for a brief moment, pressing hard against him, no doubt feeling his hardness. He again caught the scent of her herbal ointment. This time he was quite sure that it was applied for his benefit, and the realisation intensified his desire.

She then led him to the thick bush that was known as a haven for lovers in the Chief's household. It did not bother him that she hadn't said anything at all. He knew it was because she did not want to be overheard by eavesdroppers. They would spread it around that the chief's most-loved wife was having an affair with his most trusted errand boy. It would be a scandal of dire consequences. Mwangangye would then be sent away and he; he would most definitely pay the ultimate price for his indiscretions.

As soon as they got to the bush, she let go of his hand and retrieved an old mat from the thicket; Ohemba realised she had pre-prepared their meeting and the thought made him shiver with excitement. She spread the mat on the grass, knelt down and opened her arms to him. He did not need a second invitation. He undid the buttons of his shorts and they dropped to his ankles; then he covered her body with his. He wrapped his muscular arms around her and crushed her into the mat. The world stopped the moment he was engulfed by the moist warmth of her core. *I have done it*, he thought. *She is even better than I thought*. He was ecstatic.

Then after the happiest five minutes of his life, Ohemba heard someone calling him. He tried to ignore the person, praying that whoever it was would give up and go away. But the person was persistent, and refused to go. But wait a minute! That voice! It sounded like

Mwangangye's. His Mwangangye. But it couldn't be. She was lying in his arms, contented and happy.

"Ohemba you rogue, where are you?" the voice called again.

I must be having a nightmare. He thought. As he tried to get up and pull on his shorts the voice came closer, too close for comfort.

"Ohembaaa!

One leg had successfully found its way into the much loved pair of shorts when someone pushed him violently from behind.

"How dare you take advantage of poor Kente." Mwangangye raged.

"Kente? But...b...but you..." He stammered as he tried to cover his nakedness.

In his confusion, Ohemba turned to look at the figure that was, for the first time, uncovering its face. As he turned, his eyes fell on Kente, Mwangangye's maidservant. Kente who had accompanied Mwangangye the day she was first brought to the village as the chief's wife. Kente, who suffered from a strange ailment. The disease had robbed her of an ear and seriously disfigured her nose. Both her eyes were crossed and everybody shunned her. Everybody except Mwangangye; who seemed to have a special kind of liking for Kente. It was Kente that Ohemba had just slept with. Mwangangye, his Mwangangye had tricked him.

"Now listen to me you fool. Kente might not be pretty but she is my sister."

"Your sister?"

"Shut up. I'm only telling you because you are going to be my brother-in-law."

"What?"

"You will never tell anyone that she is my sister. But tomorrow, you will go to the chief and beg his permission to marry her. You cannot leave her after what you have just done to her."

"But—"

"Shut up, will you? You may be my sister's husband-to-be, but you are still an errand boy and so you can only respond to my questions. Am I making myself clear?"

Ohemba nodded. He remembered to keep his head bowed.

"If you ever mistreat her in any way, you will have the chief to answer to. And if you think you are going to refuse to marry her, you better think twice. I will let the chief know that you have been looking at me suggestively. Now get out of my sight."

As Ohemba went through the bushes he heard Mwangangye telling Kente "We have done it. You will have a husband like all normal girls. Your troubles are over. He is a fine young man and he will treat you well."

Well, he thought miserably as he wondered what his mother would think of her daughter-in-law; *at least I'm getting Mwangangye's sister. And Sleeping with one's sister-in-law has been known to happen. Through Kente, I will one day get to Mwangangye. She won't be able to resist me. It's only a matter of time before she comes to me, just like they all do.*

While the thought that he would one day get Mwangangye was appealing to Ohemba, he still had to figure out how to explain his choice of wife, to his mother.

Lifting the Stone

Maren Bodenstein

Greylingstad – November 2004

The rains have finally come to Greylingstad - the veld is breathing and the koppies are seeping moisture. The drought is broken.

Before the rains a thousand beetles festively rise ready to feed on the promise of plenty.

David would have been happy. Not about the beetles but about the rain.

Drought and rain seem so much part of our stories. But that is not what this story is about. I want to tell you about Greylingstad and freedom. About what happens in this place on the margins, ten years after the stone was lifted off the country, about our awkward recovery as we crawled out from under the stone.

David Mqadi and I kept blaming each other for the seeds not germinating. Even easy things like radishes, cabbage and beetroot didn't make it. But now in hindsight I think it might have been the heat, and the late frost, and the restless winds. David said the seeds I bought were rubbish and I suspected that he had planted them wrong and didn't water them enough.

"Did you use that compost I bought?" I ask him tersely.

"If I put any more into this soil the plants are going to burn," he grumbles and mutters in his old man ways something like, "You with your city ways, what do you know about planting?"

My city ways tell me that I pay my gardener to water and weed and keep things tidy, so that I, who is busy earning a living but yearn to garden, can experience the joy of planning and planting. But David sees things differently. He likes to collect seeds and cuttings all over the village. If you want granadillas, he will find fruit in someone's garden and rear plants from pips. And when I bring seeds from the expensive garden shops in Jo'burg he quickly plants them before I can stop him; and then he pretends that he can't remember where he planted them and hides the rest or passes them on to one of the other ladies he works for.

A few weeks ago, David announced that he wanted to plant green beans. So I obliged him by buying seeds and planting them myself. Unlike everything else, they came up beautifully in the drought, but David simply ignored them and conjured up his own bean seeds.

Beans do well in Greylingstad. But not much else seems to flourish.

In the 1880's, when everybody else was finding gold in Johannesburg, the founding fathers too discovered a nice thick reef of the stuff running under the koppies. In their happy haste to build another City of Gold they gave Greyling the title of 'stad,' but it turned out that this reef was too broken to mine. A few years later, the whole old Stad had to be moved off the koppies because President Paul Kruger refused to bring closer the railway line he was building between Johannesburg and Durban.

But at least then the place was still on the R23 which takes travellers to the uglier parts of the country. You should have seen it in those glory days. There were four petrol stations and proper places where you could sit down and eat. They even built an imposing sandstone church for the wealthy farmers in the area.

But in the 1980s, Greylingstad suffered another blow – a bypass was built, so that hasty travellers did not have to stumble over our one and only stop street anymore.

So today if your car breaks down here, all you will do is curse. The petrol station has dangerous potholes and the attendants seem to prefer it if you do not disturb their cheerful peace. And should you get hungry, you will have to snoop among the dented tins at the One Price shop or the bicycles and mielie meal at Solly's. There is butchery where you can get a decent piece of raw meat and a funeral undertaker if things really take a turn for the worse.

Should you have any curiosity left, you could look around and see that you have landed in a typical apartheid village with its white suburb against the koppies, and the smoky black township in the muddy vlei below. You might even see the ruins of the old Stad in the koppies.

After the good burghers moved Greylingstad the few kilometres closer to the railway line, they assigned the old Stad to the blacks. Then, in the year of *Our Democracy*, 1994, they changed their minds again and moved everybody from the old Stad into a township they had built with typical small four-roomed houses and grid patterned streets. On the outskirts of the township, you will find what you find all over the rural areas in South Africa - the tin makukus of the farm labourers who were retrenched when the laws on minimum wages changed.

But I ramble on. This is the problem with villages. There is a story behind every stone and it is hard to know when to stop.

What I did want to tell you is that David died last week. Before the big rains. He had a stroke.

And you know the last time he came to work he was so cheerful. For a moment I thought it had something to do with Christmas coming and bonuses, but then I felt bad about thinking that and immediately gave him the packet of squash seeds I had kept to myself.

When I phoned Ria, one of the other women he worked for, to tell her the news, she could hardly speak.

The next day I meet her in front of the bank in Balfour and it is terribly hot and I don't know her well enough to hug her.

"I don't know why I can't stop crying," she says.

"Me too." And we quickly dissolve in the heat in front of the bank, shedding tears for a gardener who collected seeds and plants and distributed them amongst the lonely white ladies of Greylingstad.

But generally there's not that much love floating around this place. People have come here because life is hard and rent and land are cheap. For some reason, there are quite a few manless women living here - each with her own story, which most probably contains some useless man. Maybe we feel safe in Greylingstad.

Most of the men don't have work. Some have found work hundreds of kilometres away and come home once a month. There's not so much to do anymore for an unskilled white man these days. My neighbour, Danie du Toit, is one of those who were retrenched from the mines years ago. And although he is getting on in life, you can see that he misses work. He is constantly on the lookout for odd jobs. And even though he does not trust Solly - the wealthy and unpopular shopkeeper who plays Radio Allah all day long - Danie cannot resist the offer of work.

When he doesn't have work he tidies his garden. All day long, I see him with his shirt off in the blazing sun - he likes to be brown. So brown that he looks like a piece of biltong.

Somehow, when I first moved here two years ago, Danie and his family did not really know what to make of this woman from Johannesburg. Even though the city is only a hundred kilometres away, they have never been to that Sodom and Gomorrah. So instead of a welcoming melktert, the wife soon sent Danie across with the message that if my dog ever shat on her lawn again he would be sjambokked.

Until I had the fence put up, their son, bored, obese and unemployed, frequently frightened this skittish city woman with his unannounced visits. He would sit himself down in my lounge uninvited and tell stories of crime and danger designed to make me fearful and needy, while neglecting to tell me that the two white boys who were responsible for much of the petty thieving in the town three years ago, had been safely locked up. He did warn me not to trust the little berry pickers from the township who were definitely sent into the koppies to spy on us. Besides, no self-respecting person walked in the veld. If I didn't stop that habit soon, he warned me, my dog would surely die of tick bite fever. And not only were the ticks in our veld particularly lethal, but the place was also riddled with cobras and adders.

That is probably why the white men seem only to walk in the veld on Sunday afternoons - feeling pissed-off after the family lunch, I imagine they want to instil a bit of manhood in their sons or grandsons by shooting at birds and porcupines and meercats and snakes.

Nature has to know its place here in Greylingstad.

And that includes the jackals.

I remember the first night in my little house on the edge of the koppies. It was icy cold and I felt unexpectedly forlorn - I hadn't bargained on the impenetrable darkness and the little creatures scurrying around the house and the owl hooting in the tree nearby. Ah, but when I lay snugly in my bed and heard the jackals calling to each other in the neck of the koppies, I felt the shiver of adventure and wildness and I knew that I had fallen in love.

The next weekend three of my nephews came to visit. I was cooking supper inside while they were making a fire, drinking sherry and admiring the star smitten sky.

Suddenly, I heard some shots and soon the boys stumbled giggling into the kitchen.

'What happened?'

They told me that Danie had walked up to the fence with his gun, slightly intoxicated, asking where I was.

"In the kitchen," they replied politely.

"Tell her that she mustn't be afraid if I shoot," he said.

"As long as you don't shoot us," they retorted wittily.

No, he was just shooting into the air to warn off the jackals.

Again I felt so forlorn. How could I explain to my only neighbour about the thrill of jackals calling in the night?

But now Danie and I have become friends. He gives me advice over the fence on how I too could turn this 'my' lily-white body brown, and I tell him that I don't want to look like him, skinny and dry like a piece of biltong. He brings the occasional basket of beans or loquats from his tidy garden and sometime this year he seems to have stopped using the word 'kaffir'.

You see, just as I loved jackals, Danie loves work, and so when I wanted to put up a fence to keep his son out, he was the obvious man for the job.

David and he had worked well together. All day long Danie talked and joked while David humoured him. Then, there was the veranda to be fixed and my roof to be painted. Two old men sitting on the roof surveying the valley below, smoking and scheming how, when the job was done, they could get a beer and some meat out of me.

When David died, the first person I wanted to tell was Danie. He wasn't home when I ran to the fence like an inconsolable child. Instead I met his son.

"Ag shame." His voice was cold.

When Danie came back he didn't say anything, he just went straight into my garage to finish all the jobs that David had alerted him to.

It must be a year ago now, the spring was hot and dry like this one; everyone was predicting the worst drought ever - villages are full of hyperbole. So when the rains did finally come, I ran into the koppies to meet the cold thick drops - my dog was with me when a shrill whistle alerted us to a herd of rheebuck. There were eight of them, young ones too. They stopped to look at us. And then the rain came down hard and they scurried off higher into the thickets.

My heart leapt and I wanted to run after them at breakneck speed over the koppies and far away to where the wild things are.

Now Phillip Ngomezulu also loves the koppies. Beyond all reason. He grew up with David in the old Stad where they played and roamed the veld together, herding cattle, hiding from bad-tempered white men and their sjamboks, collecting berries and hunting rabbits and guinea fowl. In those days they used to call the koppies the medicine hills because they are so rich in muti plants.

But Phillip's life took a different turn to David's, which probably had something to do with coming from a prominent family while David's father had arrived in Greylingstad from the Transkei to help build the railway line. But that is another story.

Phillip is a handsome chap. When he was sixteen he made a girl pregnant. To save the honour of the family, he was promptly banished to Johannesburg where he received a good education and participated in liberation politics. In 1963 he was locked up for three months in the Old Fort for *furthering the aims of communism*.

Phillip worked hard to raise his four children in those turbulent years and made sure that they all got a university education. But like many men of his generation, who did not foresee that freedom was quite so close, he drank a bit too much. So, when it was time to retire, his children threatened him with another banishment:

"Old drunkard," they chided, "go back to that Greylingstad place of yours, and leave us to take care of our mother."

The threat worked. Philip stopped drinking and built himself a house of stone and thatch in his beloved Greylingstad. His wife joined him. When they arrived here five years ago no one brought a welcoming melktert. Just the old mistrust.

"'What do you want here, old man?" the people asked.

Can't they see? Phillip wants to rest amongst the koppies, keep livestock, plant mielies and vegetables. He has even put in a land claim for the old Stad to be returned to the people. But he does not get much support for this idea - many remember how hard life was there without water and electricity - instead, they have hired lawyers from Johannesburg to apply for restitution money from the government. He speaks angrily about this when he visits me on his way back from tending to his cattle in the koppies.

But a few weeks ago, Phillip arrived at my house in a buoyant mood. He had just come from the police station - Hannes Botha the dairyman had impounded his cattle for straying onto church-land and the two old men had nearly come to blows. Luckily, our police commander has recently been on a workshop to learn mediation skills. It must have been a long session; arguing over grazing rights and fences and boundaries, but it all ended with Phillip's triumphant: "Once and for all Botha, tell me, who made you king of Greylingstad?" said the station commander, ordering Hannes to return the cattle.

The first time I met Hannes I had been sitting peacefully at my desk, when a bakkie came tearing up the hill and stopped right in front of my house.

A short, red-faced man jumped out: "Where is Miems Prinsloo?"

"I live here now," I replied calmly.

He lifted his cap to wipe down the unruly wisps of white hair. It was a hot day. "Have you seen my peacocks?"

I was flummoxed. Even though I do secretly see myself as the gatekeeper of the koppies, I never imagined these exotic birds strutting about in the long grass.

Apparently Hannes had acquired them over the weekend in Standerton and they had escaped overnight into the dominee's sheep kraal.

"They are not used to cattle," explained Hannes. "They know sheep."

I told him I would keep a look out.

He jumped back into his bakkie and rode off over the yellow hypoxis, the delicate purple flowers, the fresh grasses that survived the drought and the stampede of the cattle wars.

I invited Phillip over for a celebratory cup of herb tea. When he arrived, David was working outside. We chatted about Hannes who leaves bakkie tracks all over the veld and imagine how his hands must be itching for the olden days when people still knew their places. Phillip borrowed a book on medicinal plants and we talked endlessly about protecting our vegetables from the ravages of beetles.

"Why don't you visit me more Mqadi?" Phillip called out to David as he left.

David smiled and continued to garden.

If you lift the stone off the country you find all kinds of goggas crawling out. Some plants might never recover from their misshapen beginnings; others struggle in their crocked, yellow way.

Yesterday when it started to rain I went walking in the koppies with my dog again hoping to meet the herd of buck. But all I could find was a feeling of unease. And then, holding my head low against the icy drops, I saw the hacked off foot of a buck on the path, the grizzly job of a poacher and I sat down in the rain and sobbed.

Why do you tell these half truths about old men in Greylingstad when the buck are being killed and bakkies arrive on weekends to plunder the medicines on these hills? I chided myself. Why don't you tell about the politician who is bragging about international contracts to finally mine the koppies? How can you speak about the delicate veld and not about the hopes of the young for jobs and prosperity? Why do you ignore the dream that gave birth to this place, that one day it will be swallowed by a city larger than Johannesburg?

Because all I want is to be left alone to lick my wounds and stare into the distance; for a while to grow into the wild woman who roams the medicine hills with porcupine quills in her hair, telling implausible stories and calling to the jackals to beware of the grumpy old men who argue about seeds and cattle.

Because it's raining and David is dead and I want to show him how well the squashes have come up. I want to see him walking up the hill slowly with seeds in his pockets, whistling hymns; hear the dog's joyful yelp of recognition.

Because freedom is a trickster who, just before the rains, triumphantly releases a thousand beetles ready to feed on the promise of plenty.

And it's raining, it's raining, it's raining in Greylingstad.

The Pot

Angella Emurwon

Plants yawned and stretched. Leaves and branches moved languidly in the fading evening; pores and cells sated by the strength and power of the equatorial sun. Oyunai imagined it was how trees got taller. They stretched up to the sun and liked it so much that they never returned to their previous height. He liked walking down from the police post to the police barracks in the cool of the day. A path of red dirt created a maze through the sugar cane fields, and for the fifteen minutes it took to get to his hut, he would lose himself in the world his science teacher had created in his mind many innocent years ago.

Oyunai imagined plants wiping dust from old briefcases; field rats, beetles and snakes hurrying to their posts for the serious work of the night. And as the night wore on, a sugary mist would waft back and forth above the sugar cane fields, as conclusive as any work report ever prepared by a desk clerk. He could almost see the satisfied swell of sharp edged leaves as dirty barefoot children chewed and sucked on pieces of stolen sugar cane. Oyunai liked the idea that plants like humans had their own thoughts, pleasures, and ambitions.

On a different day, he would have chosen a random turn and walked a little longer inside the sugar cane fields but he needed to find a permanent solution to the contentious issue of the pot, before Maria made good on her threats to leave him and take their unborn child with her. They had waited a long time for this child.

Ah, women. His old science teacher should have devoted some time to the study of women. Maybe like the plants that often occupied his imagination on this daily walk, he would find a theory that helped him make sense of what happened when a woman got an idea in her head.

Akello, Maria's younger sister, had come to visit a few weeks back bearing the pot as a gift. Its presence in their home made every other possession they had seem old and worthless. Akello had taken the pot out of a frilly pink pillowcase which she casually dropped to the dusty floor; and what a pot! Delicate little pink and blue flowers followed silver rings round the coated surface creating a pastel garden. The pot was rimmed with a silver band as were both handles at its sides. It sat fat and rounded in Akello's hands as she held it out to Maria, who turned away and busied herself with something else. Oyunai knew that it would be unwise to take the pot so he too found something else to do.

Akello had done well in school and then in marriage when Hajji, a house-ware merchant in Kampala, paid fat healthy cows to make her his third wife. Hajji had recently returned from a buying trip in Dubai where he had bought Akello a new set of pots. So Akello decided to give Maria her old pot, now that she was in cast iron. It was a gesture Oyunai found thoughtful and generous, but Maria did not. Maria was slighted: slighted by the headache inducing perfume that announced Akello's presence, slighted that despite good qualifications, Akello was content to waste her life on boiling bath water for Hajji and fleeting over the fence gossip, slighted by the nonchalance of Akello's fingers as they riffled through bank notes in her *real-real leather* Dubai purse, slighted by her younger sister presenting an almost new pot as a cast away.

The pot remained above the cupboard where Oyunai had put it after he picked it off the floor. Akello had found herself holding out the pot to no one in particular and perhaps confusion slackened her hands and it fell to the floor despite her attempt to try and catch it. They watched it clank and roll, back and forth, until it settled still on the floor and the room fell strangely silent.

For the three days Akello squeezed her perfume drenched self and her belongings into their one room hut, she marvelled at how her sister could do so much with such a *cute-cute policeman hut*. All the while, Maria cooked and served food in her misshapen kerosene-blackened saucepans.

The sisters spent their time on nostalgic retellings from their younger years. Maria nostalgically recounted their childhood adventures as Akello curled her feet under her voluminous shift dress and gathered the folds with her sister's voice into herself. In those moments Maria relaxed until it was time to cook or serve food, then it seemed as if the pot would grow in the room and call attention to itself, an eager student with the right answer.

Akello soon returned to Kampala. Before her perfume had dissipated from where it clung to the bed sheets, sewn together and hung as a curtain separating their bed from the small semi-circle that was the rest of the house, Maria told Oyunai to get rid of the pot. Oyunai's attempts to reason with her only got him the silent treatment. When he said that they should perhaps sell the pot because it looked like it could bring in some money, Maria scoffed and began boiling a handful of unsalted beans in the pot as his supper.

Now she had declared that she would not live in the same house as the pot. So Oyunai had hidden the pot under the pile of dirty clothes that was accumulating at the foot of the bed. He was the one washing the clothes now because Maria was heavily pregnant. So the pot was safe in its hiding place until he could come up with a better plan.

As Oyunai approached his hut, he made out Mama Boy's squat frame in the fading light next door. Her son, Kilement Boy, was a police sergeant. Boy's teacher wife was in Kampala doing a refresher course so he had asked his old mother to come and watch his five young children until his wife's return. So far, Boy's wife had been in Kampala for two and a half years, a fact Mama Boy lamented to anyone who lingered more than a moment at her door. The youngest was now four years old and still the mother was reading books in Kampala.

"Allo! Afisa, I have your key here." Maria insisted on leaving the key with Mama Boy. Oyunai insisted on leaving the key on the back window ledge. "Maria should not still be working in her condition."

"It is what she wants."

"And at that place? Tsk tsk tsk...."

"It is what she wants."

"Eee, but you are her husband. You must wear the trousers in your house. Eeish!"

Mama Boy began to clap her hands; clicks of the tongue punctuated each clap. Oyunai knew she was about to launch a lament about Kilementi Boy's inability to wear the trousers in his own home. Boy had taken to drink in his wife's absence which added another verse to Mama Boy's laments. Oyunai murmured the usual *eeiys and eehs* as he tried to fish his keys from her clapping hands. His fingers connected with the ball of his 2010 FIFA World Cup key holder and with a flick of his wrist the key slipped out of Mama Boy's hand.

Oyunai quickly unlocked the padlock, slid back the bolt and let the door swing open. The uni-port was one of many identical round tin huts that dotted police stations across the country. Like the others, *his kibaati*, had begun life in a shiny galvanized village but it rapidly browned into rust-crusted domesticity. Each uni-port had two windows, a door, and a patch of yard outside the door opening up to a circular courtyard. A row of shared mud walled bathrooms and pit latrines stood a little way off, like an afterthought.

Inside the hut Oyunai was assailed by the acrid fumes of the paraffin stove. Maria had cooked inside the house again knowing he hated it. The sun burnt the *kibaati* from the outside and the stove heated the *kibaati* from the inside making it impossible to think, let alone sleep even hours after the sun had gone down. He imagined it was what it felt like to be baked in an oven. He left the door open so the evening air would chase away the kerosene fumes and cool the inside of the hut. This was an open invitation to vicious mosquitoes that could bite through blankets. But at least now that Maria was heavily pregnant, they had bought a treated mosquito net.

Feeling along the window ledge and finding the box of matches, Oyunai lit a match to a candle and immediately his heart sank.

The pot sat; fat and accusing, on the low table in the middle of the room. The heat from its contents created sweaty buds of condensation on its sides, which grew into each other and ran down the side of the pot to form a puddle on the table. Oyunai hesitantly lifted the pot lid and inside was half a handful of boiled beans.

Oyunai looked at the time. If Maria returned from the village bar where she worked before he had dispensed of the pot, it would not just be a quarrel, it would be Big Fight Day!

Oyunai had two hours before she returned. First, he lifted the pot off the table, carried it outside and set it on the ground. Second, he found the basin under their bed with the floor rag, and wiped the puddle from the table. He threw the rag under the bed and pushed the basin back in front of it. Next, he blew out the candle, bolted the door behind him and snapped the padlock shut. He then stuffed the keys into his pocket. He'd be back before her anyway.

Outside, he emptied the contents of the pot over a nearby bush and hurried back through the sugar cane fields to the main road. He had no time to notice the scurrying sounds in the undergrowth, nor hear for the owl that hooted from an unseen tree, no time to marvel at the blackness of the sky that made the few visible clouds look like brushes of blue-grey gauze. His mind made and discarded plans. Maria would want details; what did he do with the pot, was it gone for good or would she bump into it at the neighbours or when visiting friends? She would want something that would sooth the irritation she felt for Akello's opulent, un-ambitious life.

Oyunai kept coming back to the conclusion that if they could not keep the pot, then the next best thing was to sell the pot, but to whom? He could now hear the approaching whine and vroom of traffic on the main road. It would not be the easiest thing to stop a passing motorist and offer the pot for sale. What he needed was a traffic offender, someone who wouldn't dally with the details. He knew the perfect place to trap a speeder, the junction at Sugar, which was what everyone called the sugar factory. The road came down a steep slope, round a sharp bend, and straight into a busy junction. It came out of nowhere particularly because nearby villagers kept stealing the *Black Spot* signs to make saucepans and doors.

Having decided what to do, Oyunai's good mood was restored. He would sell the pot and use a little of the money to buy some chicken for supper and some of that roasted gizzard that Maria liked so much.

He hadn't been at the junction ten minutes before a Toyota Super Custom van flew down the hill to the waiting palm of his hand held high above his head. He smiled at the driver's confused expression as she decided; to stop or not to stop. Firstly, the khaki brown of his uniform, indicated he was not a traffic policeman. Secondly, it was too early to be checking drunk drivers. It was an intermediate hour when traffic policemen left the road to get a bite to eat before the drunks and late night speeders were on the road. And finally, Oyunai was sure the driver could make out the pretty pot he held in his other hand.

But he was resolute. He held a stern expression, held his palm up higher and stepped a little further into the road. The driver could not mistake him now. Just when Oyunai thought the driver was going to try and zoom past, brakes screeched, sprayed loose stones and dust and the vehicle stopped just before him. The driver was a woman Oyunai noticed as he approached the vehicle. As he had watched his traffic colleagues do countless times, Oyunai walked around the vehicle slowly. He studied the vehicle insurance registration on the back window, walked round the passenger side to the front making a show of reading the assorted stickers on the windscreen and then finally made his way to the driver's window.

"Eh, madam you are in such a hurry that you want to crash into me?"

"No officer, I was not that fast."

"Ah, I'm sure it was more than fifty. This is a fifty kilometres per hour zone."

"I'm so sorry. I didn't know that." Her voice trembled a little, she was fidgety.

"Is there a problem?"

"No Sir."

"Please turn on the light."

"It doesn't work. I'm just on my way to fix it."

Oyunai temporarily forgot about the pot. The Super Custom had not yet lost its new car smell, how could the cabin light not be working? He walked round the vehicle once more. This time not for show, now he was really curious. That's when he noticed the blood. The left side of the front grill was spattered with blood, so were the fog lights, as he bent his head closer he saw that bits of blood mixed with soil and plants caked a mud flap.

Unable to contain herself the driver opened her door. The cabin light sent a beam across to the other side of the road.

"Madam, you have started on the wrong foot. Lies."

"Officer, I didn't mean to do it."

"My friend, this is serious."

Oyunai straightened himself up and peered at the woman. The vehicle had made her seem taller than she was. She wore a loose fitting blouse over trousers that held her like a second skin. The hands that gripped the vehicle door were small and most probably soft. Even from where he stood he could smell the money. But he had not bargained on a long drawn out police case. This would take all night. All he wanted was a little peace and quiet after a hard day at work.

"Did the person die?"

"Person? Oh! No no, it was a goat."

"A goat?"

"Yes. It is in the boot."

"You have a dead goat in your boot?"

"Yes officer."

Oyunai burst into laughter. He laughed until his sides hurt. The driver explained that she had been speeding a little when a goat meandered into the road. She tried to swerve, but as the goat tried to get out of her way, it ran to the very side she was swerving. And then it was dead. She tried to pull the goat out of the road and into the bushes but panicked when she thought she might be found by the owner, so she had dragged the goat into her boot and driven off. Her *very designer* sweater was ruined.

> "First of all, I'm going to arrest this goat. Then, I should arrest you also for speeding, then killing, then stealing…"

As he spoke, Oyunai dragged the goat down from the boot and placed it on the ground a little impressed that this soft woman had managed to pull the goat into the boot. He could now see the dirt and blood on her trousers.

> "Please officer. I panicked. I will go back and explain."

> "After hit and run? No madam, you know the language we must speak here."

Her reply came quickly. "I don't have money."

> "The way you didn't have a light? Ok, let's go to police."

Oyunai knew these soft women never wanted to go to police. He closed the boot as she walked back to the driver's side. Reaching to the floor of the passenger side, she pulled up her handbag and retrieved a Dubai purse just like Akello's. Her face fell as she studied its contents. He knew it meant she had no small notes. Sighing she pulled out some notes and threw her handbag back to the floor. She held out a fifty thousand shilling note to Oyunai.

> "Ah, madam, but have you ever bought a goat?"

She produced another fifty thousand shilling note from her other hand.

"This is all I have."

"It is not true but it is OK. Now drive slowly, eh? We want you to reach."

The woman slowly looked at him from his standard issue boots to the soft felt of his cap and back down again. She pursed her lips and expressed in sibilants squeezed through her teeth exactly what she thought of him and his wanting her to reach; then she walked back to her car. Oyunai knew she had just bought the right to her disdain so he just smiled back at her.

He considered giving her the pot for goodwill but he knew she would toss it out of the window and probably hit him in the face with it. Besides, the pot had earned the right to call his *kibaati* its home. He folded the crisp fifty thousand shilling bills into his pocket, hoisted the goat on to his shoulders and started for home.

Maria had not yet returned. He dropped the goat outside the hut, unlocked the padlock, slid the bolt aside, entered the Kibaati, and felt for the box of matches once more. When he could see, he took off his uniform draped it over the curtain of sheets, that divided one room into two, and wore an old tee shirt and a pair of shorts. He retrieved a knife from the corner Maria had made into a kitchen and set to work.

He sharpened the knife on the *kibaati's* stone foundation until it drew blood when he pressed it against his thumb. Using the basin from under the bed as a bowl, he made short work of the goat: cut off its head, skinned it; scooped out the intestines and other edible organs, before setting to work dividing up the meat. Sweat trickled down his neck and back, soaking his tee shirt. Goat blood and hair and faeces caked his arms and legs. Flies soon invited themselves to the party but Oyunai kept going. He would be sore tomorrow but tonight he could wear the trousers in his house.

Water came next. Jerry cans of water Maria paid neighbourhood youths to carry from the main tap washed cuts of meat, liver, head, ribs, then Oyunai's arms and legs. He swept and picked up the discarded bits of meat and shoved them down the pit latrine. What he needed now was a charcoal stove, in fact he needed two. Their kerosene stove would not handle the work.

He separated the cuts of meat that would take them through the week into the basin and then divided the rest into two plastic bags. He started at Mama Boy's. Would she like a goat head to make soup for the children tomorrow? Her shouts of joy, hand claps, and tempered lamentations produced a charcoal stove and a small bag of charcoal. He dashed back home, lit the charcoal stove then left it outside for the coals to burn hot enough to cook. Then he went on to his other neighbourly neighbour. A goat leg ensured that Sergeant Opio was happy to lend him the use of his charcoal stove as well as the gift of a small bag of charcoal. Soon he was back at his hut where the coals on the other stove were glowing red. He split the lit coals between the two stoves and added fresh charcoal to both. He was ready to start drying huge chunks of meat so as to preserve them for their meals over the coming days.

By the time Oyunai heard the drone of the boda boda motorcycle break through the stillness of the night, a goat stew was bubbling in the redeemed pot over the kerosene stove, and a pile of charcoal dried meat was growing in the basin beside him. A yellow beam preceded the boda boda's arrival through the corridor of *kibaatis*. He watched Maria exchange money and niceties as she reclaimed her handbag from around the boda boda rider's neck. Maria waddled toward him her narrow waist thickened by his child growing within her. Five years ago, they had laughed together inside this very *kibaati* buoyed by two medium-density school issue mattresses. Oyunai had sat his O levels two years before and joined the force as soon as his results were out. Higher education was not something he had thought about. He had decided like his brother before him that the police force offered the best option of a steady income for a young man from his background.

Maria was their neighbour's daughter, young, pretty, and principled. When he had first approached her with words of love, she had told him she only spoke to boys who wore leather shoes. He worked every farm job he could find the next school holiday until he bought himself a good second hand pair of brown leather shoes. With money left over, he bought a small bottle of lotion and perfumed writing paper where he wrote a four page proposal that included the lyrics from popular songs of the day. He enclosed the lotion with his proposal and asked Akello, who was herself becoming a young woman, to run his message to Maria. The next time they met at

Sunday Service, Oyunai's shirt and trousers were pressed and his brown leather shoes shone in the sunlight. Maria thanked him for the sweet smelling lotion and asked him to write to her when she was away at school.

Watching her now, her eyes ready for battle, her clenched fists attempting to lend force and aggression to her rounded frame, Oyunai could not believe this was that same girl who had fiercely defended the life she wanted, as a young cadet's wife despite her parents urging her to complete her A levels. Maria had assured her parents that Oyunai was hardworking, a favourite of his superiors, and would soon be promoted to the Kampala Central Police Station. They would be living in glamorous Kampala in no time.

Five years later, they were still in Lugazi and she no longer laughed when they lay together on the mattress. She had found a job as a cashier in the village bar because the owner said it was easier to trust a woman with his money. Oyunai was happy because now she had her own work problems and didn't have the time to pick apart gossip about slights and promotions at the police post.

But with her modest salary came months of warding off unwanted advances from drunk customers who, when rebuffed, called her *malaya*. She asked them how it could be that she was a prostitute because she worked in a bar. A prostitute because she wouldn't accept their advances? *Malaya* because she was a married woman without children? But now that she was pregnant the same men called her mama and wondered if her husband was a real man for letting her continue to work at the bar.

Maria slowed as she neared the hut, distracted by the meat in the basin and on the charcoal stove. Then her eyes settled on the pot.

"It is still here? Then it is me who must go."

Oyunai lifted the lid and stirred. Chunks of meat broke apart in the thick stew, the aroma from the pot rising. He watched Maria swallow, shifting slightly from foot to foot; her hand rubbed her belly absent mindedly.

Oyunai disappeared into the hut and returned with two bowls and spoons. He served a generous helping of the stew into one bowl, shifted a little in the doorway where he was seated, then offered the bowl to Maria.

"You must be hungry."

Maria lowered herself gingerly to sit beside him taking the bowl. The first spoonful produced a sigh of pleasure. She followed with several quick spoonfuls. And Oyunai imagined his child yawning and stretching contentedly, warmed by the heat from the delicious stew.

Oyunai served his own bowl and they sat together eating quietly as once in a while he turned pieces of meat on the charcoal stoves. Soon all the meat was dried. He carried the basin of dried meat into the house, doused the charcoal stoves with water, and sat back down to resume his meal.

Maria's spoon clinked against the bottom of the bowl. "Kilement Boy was at the bar again today."

Oyunai nodded and exhaled inwardly. At least he had peace.

For now.

The Autopsy

Frances Naiga Muwonge

Charles Clever died on Saturday night; however, his body didn't reach the JFK Memorial Hospital morgue until Sunday morning. The village doctor had embalmed Charles in the traditional way and wrapped his corpse in an incense smoked reed blanket.

Charles' mother, the old Ma, propped atop a magenta and beige sisal mat; was tucked in a corner of the small intake room. The room was bare except for a small wooden desk along the back wall and a dented metal file cabinet with the bottom two drawers missing. On the wall, four rusted metal clasps indicated something once hung there.

Like the rest of the hospital, the intake room stank; a vile cocktail of human emissions. The stench was heightened by the tropical air and water-logged ceiling, a consequence of the protracted rainy season. The old Ma's normally towering figure was lost in drapes of fabrics all of brown and black hues. The wrappers were gifts from mourners, strangers and well-wishers she had encountered as she accompanied her son's body from the village to the hospital in the capital. Her bosom was mapped with white flaky stains from her tears and running nose. The old Ma rocked her body back and forth flaring her angular nostrils with each breath she took. She threw her head forward until her fleshy chin smacked against her pillow like chest; then, bellowing her dead son's name, she threw her head back heavily until it rested painfully against the top of her spine.

Charles' favourite Aunt Fatou, the old Ma's much younger sister, couldn't sit still. She fluttered between consoling the old Ma and her remaining nephews, Abraham and Abdou.

Every one ignored Anna, Charles' baby mama. They had loved her in the beginning, but they had never forgiven her for leaving Charles when the NGO where he worked as a driver lost its funding. The old Ma understood Anna and Charles' break up somewhat, but Anna taking away their son Charles Junior; was inexcusable.

Anna left Charles for an accountant who worked with another international NGO - one that had just received supplementary funding for another year. The accountant was able and very willing to use his ample financial resources to lure the impressionable young mother, to the extent that when the accountant dropped the Charles and abbreviated her child's name to Junior, Anna soon followed suit.

But then Charles senior soon found another job as a driver for a wealthy Swedish business lady, and Anna resurfaced. First, she started bringing Junior around for visits. By the time the accountant's project funding ended, Anna had started visiting Charles alone – and she had resumed calling her son Charlie Junior.

To keep out of the family's way, Anna volunteered to go out and look for food.

"What! What is this! Whose body is this?" A tall nurse appeared in the doorway; her name tag read 'Kolu'. She picked at her purple acrylic nails and thrust her enormous cone-shaped breasts out as she spoke. She held a plastic Nokia phone in one hand. Her white hat was pinned onto a forest of tightly coiled synthetic curls. Her dark skin was flawless, and although beads of sweat dotted her nose, she had a polished grace about her.

The family who had been waiting for two hours were startled at the nurse's sudden appearance. The old Ma stopped mid sway and stared blankly at Kolu. The deep fissures in her cheeks indicated a frown was her usual expression.

Fatou, who was huddled over a mobile phone with Abraham, immediately abandoned him and rushed to sit by her sister.

"This is my brother Charles," Abraham Clever finally said after a pregnant pause. "We need an autopsy. Someone killed my brother. He wasn't sick, and now he is dead. He was only 36. He should not be dead."

Kolu purposefully made her way from the doorway, past Abraham, and then she paused briefly to examine the old Ma before she arrived at the small wooden desk.

"I'm very sorry for your loss, I really am, but don't you know you are not supposed to handle a corpse?" she asked, looking at Abraham.

"My brother was poisoned!" Everyone turned to look at Abdou, Charles' half –brother. He stood with his emaciated frame slouched against the door. His eyes were blood shot and he had on his just-dead brother's treasured white New Balance high tops. The scent of liquor and cigarettes filled the air seconds after he opened his mouth.

"We need proof so we can have the people at his work place arrested. They killed him," Abdou added.

Fatou rose from the mat where she sat with the old Ma and stood in front of Abdou, who always drank too much and usually misbehaved thereafter. Having grown up as siblings, she was accustomed to covering for him.

"Charles was my nephew. He *is* my nephew; but he's more like a brother to me. He had a good job, working as a driver for an important lady. His boss lady even promoted him because he did such a good job, that's why the other people at his work place got jealous and killed him." Fatou explained using her slender frame to block Abdou and keep him in the doorway.

"Who is demanding the autopsy?" Kolu slowly examined all the faces in the room. "Do you have a referral from a doctor?" she finally asked Fatou. She continued to ignore Abdou.

"He died in the village," Abraham said as he manoeuvred on the mat from his mother's side to where Charles' reed encased body lay. He was careful not to touch Charles' freshly shaved head. "We had taken him to the village for treatment. We first tried all the doctors in town but they said it was malaria. When malaria treatment didn't work, they said it must be typhoid, then Lassa fever; but his symptoms were nothing like typhoid or Lassa fever. The doctors just kept taking our money. It was like he was slowly getting paralyzed from the inside. That's when we took him to our medicine man in my old Ma's village. He died there on the fifth day. From the time he got sick he just kept getting worse until he died." As he spoke, Abraham's eyes watered, but his voice remained unshaken. However, as soon as he finished speaking, he collapsed sideways and his head landed in the old Ma's lap.

"That is terrible to hear, I cannot even imagine your grief. I am so sorry for your loss," Kolu said sympathetically, "I am sorry to ask you but…why didn't you bury him in the village?"

"Madam, I'm telling you my nephew was poisoned and we need proof!" Fatou said moving closer to the Nurse's table. The old Ma had stopped rocking her head back and forth violently and was now humming a tune through clenched teeth.

Abdou stepped forward, but Fatou side stepped and positioned herself before him and she said, "We are not rich people but she has the money to pay for an autopsy." Fatou pointed at the old Ma. "The police told us the autopsy is thirty thousand Shillings. Please do an autopsy. We will pay."

"Why are you certain he was killed? There are many reasons a young man can die. He doesn't have to be sick to die. Maybe it was God's will," Kolu said ignoring her Nokia phone which rang until it cut.

Before anyone could answer Kolu, Anna entered, "I found us some breakfast - beignets and bread, plus I have things for tea; someone lent me a flask so I managed to bring hot water," she announced, feeling pleased with her contribution to the effort.

"And who is this?" Kolu asked, examining Anna with the kind of disapproval women often reserve for other woman they deem to be of similar or more attractiveness than themselves.

Kolu paused to observe Anna, then she smirked when she noticed that Anna's synthetic hair was of low quality, and that her pale green bra showed through the sheer white blouse she wore over electric blue leggings.

"I'm Charles' lady, we have a son together," Anna began before Abdou interrupted.

"You were not his woman, you left him remember. You are only his son's mother. That's all."

"Isn't that what I said?" Anna snapped. "I'm the mother of his only son!"

She slammed the two black plastic bags onto the Nurse's table and stomped to the back of the room. The bag with the bread and beignets landed on the table but the plastic bag filled with powdered milk wrapped in little plastic triangles, sugar, instant coffee and a few tea bags dropped to the floor; Nurse Kolu picked it up.

"Who is demanding the autopsy?" Nurse Kolu asked again, as she casually glanced through the contents of the bag. "Do you have a referral request from a doctor?"

"Madame, my son did not die. They killed him!" the old Ma spoke up from where she sat; a heap of sorrow. Everyone, including Kolu looked at the old Ma.

"This was not God's will, it was the devil! I want those boys to go to jail. I need an autopsy so I can give evidence to the police!" The old Ma's voice cracked and she was overrun by tears.

"That is what they told us, we need an autopsy! They can only arrest them if they have proof. We need an autopsy! And we have the money to pay. So what is the problem?" the old Ma asked as Fatou tried to restrain her flailing arms.

"Ma please I beg you, I know the hardest thing in the world for a mother to do is bury her child but sometimes we have to accept God's plan for us..." Kolu said as she moved from behind the desk.

"But this wasn't God's plan I beg you to hear me O!" the old Ma started wailing. A crowd of curious on lookers started to form in the corridor and another group who were gathered under a mango tree, moved towards the outside window of the room. The rest of the hospital staff continued to go about their business unconcerned; they had not been paid in two months so staff morale was very low.

Kolu dropped her phone into the tiny pocket of her starched white uniform, approached the old Ma and knelt before her.

The old Ma was now draped across her son's corpse.

"Ma, this is a hospital, there are rules and procedures. We do not just accept dead bodies. But because I understand your grief, let me see what I can do for you. Let me sort out this autopsy business. Just wait here for me." Kolu said gently patting the old Ma.

"You said you had brought the money right? You have thirty thousand Shillings with you now?" Kolu confirmed before leaving the small room.

About an hour later, Kolu returned with a young nurse and an orderly.

The new nurse looked as if she could be one of Kolu's sisters, except for the more compact physique and lighter skin. The orderly's black gum boots were covered in mud and ash. He was pushing a rusted gurney with wheels that squeaked and rattled as it moved.

"We have the clothes we want you to dress him in after the autopsy; for the funeral, you know," the old Ma gestured towards Fatou who retrieved Charles' favourite garments from where they were neatly folded in a green plastic bag.

Kolu took the bag from Fatou and handed it to the orderly who placed it on the gurney. While the younger nurse asked Fatou questions and jotted down information on a lined piece of notebook paper, Kolu ushered the old Ma to her feet. With Abraham's help, the orderly rearranged the reed blanket and placed Charles' corpse on the gurney. As they wheeled Charles away, Kolu opened out her arms and held the Old Ma in a tight embrace.

Fatou hurriedly signed every document the younger nurse presented for signature. Meanwhile, the old Ma discreetly handed Kolu the 30,000 Shillings she had knotted in a handkerchief and stuffed into her bosom.

Kolu offered a receipt, but the old Ma declined.

"We will communicate our findings to the police for you," Kolu said. Abraham and Fatou smiled back, feeling satisfied for the first time that day.

"I will contact you when we have results and then you may collect the body and prepare for burial." Kolu added.

"I thank you, really I do. You will be blessed for this kind deed. I want you to know I will be praying for you," the old Ma said to Kolu.

Anna grabbed the black plastic bags from the table as the family left the hospital and set off back to their respective homes.

By the time the gurney with Charles' body reached the crematorium, the reed blanket had been removed and the corpse was covered with a soiled sheet that was too short to cover the full body. Charles' exposed mid-section revealed the *Tommy Hilfiger* waist band of white briefs.

As they waited at the incinerator door, the orderly and young nurse admired Charles' prized G-Star jeans and striped polo shirt. As per Kolu's instructions, the young nurse dislodged the stud Charles always wore in his left ear lobe and the gold ring from his little finger ring. She then wrapped the jewellery in a small plastic bag, which she handed to Kolu together with the green plastic bag containing the burial garments.

"I'll be back," Kolu said as the orderly closed the incinerator door.

She rushed away from the crematorium, towards the taxi stand headed to the town centre.

Neither the young nurse nor the orderly responded; they exchanged worried glances, but said nothing.

Till Death Do Us Part

Nana Darkoa Sekyiamah

Today

The woman in the mirror stared back at me. I barely
recognized myself. Who is this woman wearing a lopsided
black head tie, with straggly bits of grey hair peeping out?

I used to love styling my hair. In my hey-day I
had the hugest afro ever, and I would lovingly pick at it
until it stood up high and proud. Angela Davis was my
role model. Well, more accurately, Angela Davis' hair, but
for the past 40 years, a comb has rarely passed through
mine.

Through the mirror to my left is my chest of
drawers. It is overflowing with boubous. That's all I
wear nowadays. Boubous. With my wonky hip, the loose
flowing kaftans are the only outfits that I can slip on
without asking Ekow for help.

Somehow Ekow has managed to keep all his body
parts working. Well, excluding the cancer that is steadily

eating away at his prostate. To be honest, I would much rather be eaten by cancer than be this shell of a woman with nothing else to do on her 70th birthday except sit in front of this mirror. I used to love this mirror; it was one of the many gifts my in-laws brought on my wedding day. Now the gilt has worn off, and the mirror appears to have become opaque with time, as has my marriage.

I can see my bed reflected in the mirror – a narrow frame, covered in a blue and white cloth. I didn't bother to get a bigger bed when I was forced to move to this room downstairs. I say forced, although no one made me do it. I was happy to move down here. What was the point of sleeping upstairs with him? A painful hip was the perfect excuse to stop climbing upstairs to his bed.

When Ekow and I built this house 45 years ago, I imagined that this would be one of the children's rooms. We had planned to have three children, ideally two girls and a boy. We were going to call our first daughter Asantewaa, after Ekow's Mum, name our son Papa after Ekow's Dad, and Ekow had agreed to name our second daughter, Naana, after my mother. I had decided my son would have the downstairs room because boys need their independence. Ekow, the girls, and I would occupy the three bedrooms upstairs.

We even had a guest room downstairs, but over the years Ekow converted it into a study where he now spends all his time. It's where he keeps the pictures of his other family. Well, with the exception of her. At least he has been decent enough not to flaunt her. There's a picture of Asantewaa at her graduation in London, Papa, when he had his matriculation at the University of Ghana, and Nyarkoa, when she graduated from the Kwame Nkrumah University of Science and Technology. I guess *his* dreams came true.

I wasn't always a woman with shattered dreams. I had plenty of dreams when Ekow and I met in 1959. True, I was only 16 at the time, and he was 19 but we dreamt together. We believed in Kwame Nkrumah and the United States of Africa. We were passionate about changing the continent, which was why we both wanted to work in the Foreign Service. Eventually Ekow joined the service whilst I became a teacher.

We got married on New Year's Day in 1967. He said he chose that date because he didn't want us to forget the happiest day of our lives. He said he would never let me go; that I would be his wife forever.

On that day, I got up before dawn because I was too excited to sleep. Soon after, my favourite Aunt Adwoa came into my room with her signature smile which made her eyes crinkle in the corners. She sat beside me on the mattress and said,

"My daughter this is a big day for you. Ekow is a good man. You are going to be a wife, mother and queen of your household. You are indeed blessed." She reached for my hand and I held onto it tightly.

"You know I haven't been lucky enough to be queen of my household. So I want to advise you. No matter what happens, make sure you remain the head of your household. Don't let anyone come between you and Ekow. Don't talk about your home affairs with other women, especially young women who are not yet married. You never know who is waiting to step into your shoes."

The day went by in a blur of colours and sounds. Ekow's family arrived early shouting *Agoo fia ha* repeatedly until the members of my family responded *Amee*. Ekow's family then entered the household.

I sat in my room whilst my younger cousin Amma dashed back and forth, relaying details of what was going on outside to me. The amount of fabric Ekow's family had brought – 12. The number of his relatives who turned up – at least 60. The number of gifts they came bearing – uncountable, according to Amma, who by this time had started to dream aloud about what her own wedding day would be like. Everyone *"ohhhd"* and *"ahhhd"* when I was finally brought out behind three of my friends who had been initially presented as the fake brides. The linguist representing my family sang my praises.

Ah, this our daughter, she is a beautiful flower. And she's no ordinary flower eh? We have made sure we've kept her safe from weeds. She is an obaa sima. An ideal woman, and furthermore, a modern obaa sima. Her mother and father made sure that even though she studied at university, she also learnt how to cook all the traditional foods. She can make abenkwan, nkatie kwan, and even pound and turn fufu all by herself. And can you see how beautiful she is? She is a first class beauty. A woman like this is a rare bead. She must be treasured. She must be handled gently like glass. Treated like the precious woman that she is.

Ekow's family's linguist responded in kind, reaffirming my beauty, thanking my parents for how well they had brought me up, and singing the praises of Ekow, a good looking man who had excelled at university and was serving in the Foreign Service. The linguist predicted that one day he would be a big man. And she was right.

Yesterday

Ekow and I settled into marriage bliss and time moved on. Nkrumah was exiled to Guinea. J.W.K. Harley, A.K. Ocran and A.A. Afrifa came in and then out of power. And Busia became Prime Minister in 1969. It was around that time that I started to feel as if I was slowly dying inside.

We had been married for over two years and I had nothing to show for it. Ekow's mother took to visiting me every few weeks and on every visit she made the point of saying things like, "Auntie Afua was asking me if I was coming to take care of my grandchild".

I prayed and prayed for that grandchild but each month I bled without fail. Ekow didn't seem bothered. He just smiled and said, "Don't worry Agatha; children are a blessing from God. They will come in their own good time." He seemed to have forgotten that day in 1963 when we had removed one of God's blessings. A Doctor in Pig Farm had opened my legs, reached inside with his forceps and pulled out something. I bled for three days afterwards. The memory haunted me. I often wondered if God ignored my prayers and refused to send me another blessing because of what I had done.

My child never came. When I brought up the subject of seeking help Ekow said I worried too much. "My friend Paul told me that it took him and his wife five years to fall pregnant," he said as he brushed my concerns aside.

It was easy for him. After all, he was not the one being badgered about when a child was going to come. Despite Ekow's assurances, in the third year of our marriage, I began to see specialist after specialist. In the beginning, Ekow came along with me. The doctors said his sperm was fine. So I decided that there was no need for him to keep coming to the hospital with me. After all, I was the one who had the problem. The quack doctor who had performed the abortion all those years ago had done a botched job.

Scraping the lining of my womb had caused intense scarring, which in addition to a blockage with one of my fallopian tubes meant that the chance of me conceiving was virtually impossible.

I was unaware of the damage until I went to see Dr Lamptey. I will never forget his words: "Agatha, come on, you are an educated woman. You should have gone to see a proper doctor. No woman in Ghana needs to go and see a backstreet doctor for a termination. That man gutted your insides as if you were a common pig." I remember thinking; *that's easy for you to say now. Who could I have gone to see? Which doctor in Ghana would have allowed a 20 year old girl to have an abortion without her parents' consent?* At the time, the quack was my only option.

After the appointment with Dr Lamptey I sat in my car for hours. It was only when the mosquitoes started buzzing through the half open windows that I turned the key in my ignition, and started the journey home. As I drove, it felt like the honk of every car was an accusation, *you see what you did? You killed your baby and now you think God will give you another one?* I went straight to our bedroom when I got home. I drew the curtains and jumped into bed still wearing the cream blouse with faux pearl buttons and my favourite blue A-line skirt which I had worn to the Doctors. All I wanted was some peace and quiet, but I heard Ekow's steps on the staircase approaching. The Doctor must have called him because he got into bed beside me and reached out to hold me.

He said, "Agi we will be okay, we can look at adopting a child."

I jumped up, "Ekow I will only say this once so listen and listen well. If I cannot carry a child of my own, if I cannot feel a baby grow within me, then so be it. I will not make myself a laughing stock. Everyone will say, look at the witch, she has eaten all the children in her womb and now she wants to take other people's children. No. I won't adopt another woman's child."

Ekow

I love you Agatha. I always have, and always will. This marriage has been tough on both of us. Yes I know you think, *you can talk,* because I have another family but things have not been as easy for me as it may look. For the first few years of our marriage, I really believed that we had nothing to worry about. I mean others have done what we did with no issues. I didn't even understand why you were in such a hurry for us to have children. I just wanted to relax and enjoy life with my new bride. But after that visit to Dr Lamptey, something in you changed. Nothing I did satisfied you. I suggested we adopt but you refused. Some of my relatives in the village even wanted to send us a young child to raise as our own – you know they believe that sometimes caring for a young child can make a barren woman fertile – but you did not even want to consider it.

I know you felt like you got the brunt of the constant questioning but I had my own share too. Even my drunken fool of an uncle once said to my face, "Ekow, I may not have your fancy job, but at least everyone knows that I am a real man." For once I didn't have a smart word to say to Uncle Joe, I just kept quiet and walked away.

That was five years after our marriage. Do you remember that in the sixth year a delegation came from my mother's ancestral village in Biriwa? In those days you had already started ignoring visitors so I told them you were in bed feeling unwell. They spoke amongst themselves in hushed voices. Eventually they revealed the reason for their visit; they had found me an eighteen-year-old young woman from the village. I thanked them for their kindness, and turned them away.

My mother was practically in tears. "Ah Ekow what do you want me to do? Don't you want me to carry my grandchild in my arms? Oh Ekow. What kraa has that woman done to you? Is it witchcraft or what?"

What could I say to my mother? *No Ma, my wife hasn't gone to see the juju man. It's my fault that she can't have children?*

So I kept quiet and watched you withdraw further and further away from me. And soon my relatives stopped coming to the house or inviting you to weddings, or engagements, or out-doorings. Not that you would have gone anyway. You always came home in tears on those few occasions when you felt obliged - usually because I insisted - that we attend an event as a couple.

It was almost a relief when I got posted to London, and you refused to come along. I didn't have to feel guilty every time I looked at you. And that was when I met Pokua. She attended one of the Embassy receptions. She reminded me a little bit of you – of how you were before 1969 – so full of energy, so full of life.

By then I had stopped wearing my ring. I didn't feel married anymore. I had been in London for two years and you had refused to come for a visit. On my visits to Ghana you were polite, more like a landlady who had a visiting guest than a woman whose husband had returned from a long stay overseas.

At that point, I couldn't even remember how long it had been since we had been intimate. I couldn't bring myself to lie with you when you lay there waiting for me to get it over and done with. You never voiced your discontent but I could feel it. The waves of, get it over and done with it, rose from your body over and over again. And you had started to wear those shapeless kaftans that did nothing to flatter your body. That body which I had always loved. That body you used to love to preserve.

I remember in the early days you would say to me, "your body is a temple," and force me to eat pawpaw for breakfast and boiled green plantains for lunch with a side of leafy green nkontomire. You would always insist that nkontomire be steamed and served with fresh pepper instead of being fried in palm oil.

But it all changed. Now you sit at the dining table, and eat whatever the house help puts in front of you. At night you get into bed with a bar of Golden Tree chocolate. I get it. I understand. You need comfort. You need solace. And somehow I can't provide that.

I guess I coped better because I had my job and the constant travels to distract me, whilst teaching did not seem to ignite any passion in you. I recall the one time you spoke of leaving your job and how I raised a fuss. I knew it was the only thing keeping you functioning. I didn't want you leaving your job and spending all your time in bed which was what you did all evenings and weekends.

When I met Pokua, I felt happiness return to my soul for the first time in years. She had what the French call *joie de vivre*, and I needed that life essence. I had been dead for years, sexually dead too. My friends had tried in vain to introduce me to other women. *Ekow meet x, she just finished university. Ekow do you know y? She works at z bank,* were conversations that took place all the time. But those women never appealed to me. Eventually, the guys gave up on introducing me to potential second wives, mistresses and girlfriends. But with Pokua, it was different. It was like falling in love all over again. I would leave work early and take her for tea at the Ritz. On Friday evening we would walk up the Strand, grab a pre-theatre dinner and watch a show. On weekends we would pick a market to visit and we would browse the stalls picking up little knick-knacks along the way. Pokua made my life brand new. For the first time, I saw the beauty of London; the greenery of Hyde Park, the charm that Hampstead Heath holds, even Dalston Market became special to me as we spent time there.

I started to wake up early and go running. I cut down on my drinking. I ate more fruit and vegetables. And then, I got a call from the Ministry of Foreign Affairs asking me to come home for a meeting with my Minister.

I remember that visit because I was shocked at the state you were in and the state of our house. The furniture in the dining and living rooms was covered in plastic casing with figurines, statuettes and dolls of all sizes and shapes covering every available space. The dining room felt hot and stuffy. It was clear that in my absence you rarely sat there. I remember that night you sat across from me at the table, barely lifting your head from the plate of spaghetti before you. I poured myself a scotch, neat, and downed it in one go. I definitely needed one. I poured myself a second one. I needed to feel the kick of the drink.

Do you remember the conversation we had? I just couldn't imagine us continuing the way we were. I couldn't think of how to begin so I think I said, "We have to talk". You didn't react. "We have to talk about us. We cannot continue like this. *I* cannot continue like this." You just continued to spoon spaghetti into your mouth. You wouldn't even look at me.

"Agatha, are you listening to me? I said we need to talk"

"So talk." You finally spoke

"It is clear that you are not happy. I don't know what I can do to make you happy. I have tried everything."

"Yes, Ekow you have tried everything." There was more than a hint of sarcasm in your voice. "No one can accuse you of not being the perfect man, an ideal husband."

"Agatha, I want a divorce."

I saw your eyes pop open then you composed yourself and looked straight at me. What I saw in your eyes scared me. You dropped the fork you were holding and said,

"I will never grant you a divorce. You and I are wed till death do us part."

I never brought up the subject of divorce again.

Agatha

I should have suspected something was wrong when Ekow brought up the subject of divorce. After all of those years and he thought he could just discard me like a piece of used tissue? The nerve. I should have realized there was someone else but it genuinely did not cross my mind. Not until that day when Mary from the Ministry called to say that my parcel had arrived through the diplomatic bag, and that I could pick it up anytime I was in town.

I found her occasional calls quite annoying and the visit to the Ministry of Foreign Affairs even more so. I always felt the eyes of the staff drilling through my back. I would turn around and catch someone quickly looking in the other direction, as if they hadn't been staring at me. I knew there were rumours about Ekow and I. People wondered why I had refused to join him abroad. They wondered why he didn't fool around with any of the women in the Ministry like the other senior civil servants who sometimes had two or three girlfriends.

I don't know why Ekow insisted on sending me parcels. I never wore any of the clothes he sent, but I did enjoy the packets of Swiss chocolate that he always included.

As usual the lift at the Ministry was not working, and so I walked up four flights of stairs to the office of the Administrative Manager. Mary looked up from her typewriter the minute I entered. She had this look in her eye that I couldn't quite place.

"Oh Auntie, welcome. Please sit down."

I nodded at her in greeting, and sat down.

"*Ei,* your husband has sent you something. You're lucky *o. Hmmm.*"

I continued to stare at the wall just to the right of Mary's head. The bookcase overflowed with files, papers, and folders of varied shapes and sizes. My eyes drifted back to Mary. *Why do so many of these women who work at the ministry end up bleaching their skins, and over plucking their eyebrows?*

"Auntie you should try and visit Mr Ekow sometime you know."

I looked at her but didn't say a word. She laughed nervously. "You know how it is abroad when the men travel alone."

I looked past Mary to the bookcase again. *Was that a spider that I could see on the top right hand side shelf?*

The scraping of the chair on the floor as Mary rose brought my attention back to her. I watched as she walked to the bookcase, her ample behind jiggled with each step she took. She pulled a parcel wrapped in brown paper from the topmost shelf and made her way back to me.

She handed the parcel to me silently. I stood up, gathered all of my dignity like a shawl around my shoulders, reached for the parcel, and walked out of the Ministry looking straight ahead. That was the last time I answered a call from Mary.

The next time Ekow came home and said we needed to talk I cut him off, "I'm not giving you a divorce," I said.

"I'm not asking for one. I just want you to know that I'm expecting a child with another woman. If God wills the child will be born in three months."

His words landed with a heavy blow. We were sitting at the dining table. I felt weak but with all the strength I could muster, I pushed back my chair, stood up and walked away.

I walked straight to my bedroom and into the familiar comfort of my bed. I had been expecting the day to come for the longest time. But when it came, I didn't know what to do. I didn't cry, or scream or rage about how it wasn't fair that he could have a child and I couldn't.

The next morning I woke up and acted as if I didn't feel as though Ekow had stabbed me in the heart the night before. I acted as if everything was okay.

And then, as if I hadn't suffered enough, the day before Ekow was due to return to London, one of my uncles came to visit. He had heard there was some news. I was in no doubt that everyone had heard the news. By then I had moved to the downstairs room. I told my Uncle that Ekow was the best person to ask for details. I retreated to my room. The door was slightly ajar. I heard the squeak of the sofa as my Uncle sat his heavy frame in it. I heard the clinking of glasses. I heard the gruff chuckle of male laughter and a snippet of conversation carried across to me. "You're a man Ekow, it's understandable."

Forever

Sometimes I look in the mirror and ask myself whether I should have made other choices. Should I have given Ekow a divorce when he asked for one? Perhaps I shouldn't have listened to Auntie Adowa when she said, "Kai. Who will marry a woman who can't have children? At least you're married. Stay in that marriage until your dying day". It hasn't been easy you know, having to share my husband with another woman. When he finally came back from London he brought them back and set up a house for them. He said, "I have to meet my obligations."

Ha! Who can fault a man for meeting his obligations? He is there every other day. He says he needs to spend time with his children. Who can begrudge him that? Well, I can; but that's neither here or there. At least he has always made sure I'm taken care of. He takes me to my hospital appointments now that I can no longer drive. He finds me new house helps when the young girls run off in the middle of the night. I've never lacked for anything yet I have nothing. I guess in his own way he still loves me.

I was worried when Ekow told me that he had developed prostate cancer. I shouldn't have worried about him though. Even cancer can't keep him down. He went into hospital, had some sort of procedure, wore a catheter for about a month, was confined to this house because of the radiation, and now the cancer seems to be under control.

Every so often he goes to see the Doctor; to have what they say are his PSA levels checked but apart from that, no one would guess that there was anything wrong with him. He's started going on long walks again. At 73 he is very physically fit. He's even managed to hold on to his looks. He is often described as a distinguished looking gentleman. He still likes to wear a smart shirt, and neatly pressed trousers. He visits the barber's every other week.

It makes me laugh that he insists he only goes to the other house to see his children. They are all grown-ups now and only the last one lives at home. On the evenings he is home I sit and indulge him, "Nyarkoa got a new job," he says. "Asantewaa turns 18 tomorrow." "I am bit worried about Papa, he can't seem to decide what he wants to do with his life."

Indeed *his* dreams came true. And he was right; I will be his wife forever.

Notes on Authors

 **Bananuka Jocelyn Ekochu** is an established writer of fiction and non-fiction. Her novel, Shock Waves Across the Ocean, was long-listed for the Dublin Impac Award. Her short stories and poems appear in different collections and anthologies.

Bodenstein Maren grew up in a tiny village established by German missionaries in the 1880's in rural Kwa Zulu Natal, South Africa. After school she went to live in the big bad city of Johannesburg. Here she studied English and Philosophy and has since  worked as a lecturer, editor and writer. Since 2004 she has been pulled back into the rural landscapes of South Africa which feed her soul.

 **Emurwon Angella** is a writer, award-winning playwright, stage director, and screenwriter who lives and works in Tororo, Uganda. She divides her time between the uneventful writing life of Tororo and her exciting mentoring work as a Youth and Film Project Consultant (Northern Uganda) and Screenwriting Mentor (East Africa) for Maisha Film Lab.

Naiga Frances Muwonge was born in Uganda during politically turbulent times and grew up internationally, primarily in America. After completing law school, she worked with NGOs and the UN in post conflict countries primarily focused on governance,  elections and the consumption of political information. She currently lives in Uganda, working on her debut novel manuscript and short stories. She also manages sales and business development for her family's organic chicken farm when not engaged in writing or consulting on governance related projects

 **Namukasa Glaydah** is a Midwife and writer, and is currently chairperson of the Uganda Women Writers' Association, Femrite. She is the author of one novel, The Deadly Ambition,

2006. Her young adult novella Voice of a Dream was awarded the Macmillan Writers Prize for Africa in 2006. Her short stories are published in anthologies in Uganda, South Africa, the UK, the US and Sweden. She is a recipient of the Rockefeller Foundation Bellagio Center Residency 2013, Mike and Marylee Fairbanks fellowship 2006, and in 2008 was awarded the title of Honorary Fellow by the International Writing Program University of Iowa. She was selected on the Africa39 list. She is currently completing her second novel.

Nana Darkoa Sekyiamah explores the diverse sexualities of African women in her writing. She is a Co-Founder of 'Adventures from the Bedrooms of African Women', a highly acclaimed and widely read blog on African women and sexuality at www.adventuresfrom.com.

Nana has also written non fiction including a *'Communications Handbook for Women's Rights Organisations'*, is co-author of *'Creating Spaces and Amplifying Voices: The First Ten Years of the African Women's Development Fund'*, and editor of *'Women Leading Africa: Conversations with Inspirational African Women'*. She has written for a number of magazines and websites including BBC Focus on Africa, The Guardian, New African Woman, This is Africa and DUST magazine.

Tidjani Antoinette Alou Born and raised in Jamaica, Antoinette Tidjani Alou is a professor of French and Comparative Literature at the Abdou Moumouni University in Niamey, Niger. She is also a citizen of Niger where she has resided permanently since 1991. A  published scholar and translator, she has finally decided to come out as an author of poetry, short stories and life writing. She loves gardening, cooking, hanging out with her girlfriends and a good workout at the gym.

Wame Molefhe Wame Molefhe is a writer living in Botswana.